Twayne's United States Authors Series

Sylvia E. Bowman, *Editor*

INDIANA UNIVERSITY

St. John de Crèvecoeur

ST. JOHN DE CRÈVECOEUR

by

THOMAS PHILBRICK

St. John de Crèvecoeur by Thomas Philbrick is the first book-length study in English of the author of *Letters from an American Farmer* to appear in more than fifty years. Crèvecoeur has long been recognized as an important contributor to the European idea of America, as an influential celebrator of the pleasures of rural life, and as an engaging delineator of American nature, but the full extent and true character of his literary achievement have never before been explored by a critical examination of the whole body of his writings.

Through an analysis of the themes and forms of the *Letters,* the other English sketches, and the later French works, Professor Philbrick traces the shifting emphasis of Crèvecoeur's thought and the radical changes in his technique over the course of his entire literary career. The portrait which emerges is that of a writer obsessed by the meaning of the American experience, one to whom the New World figured both as idyll and as nightmare. The central contention of the book is that the artistry with which Crèvecoeur rendered that complex image entitles him to a place in the first rank of American prose writers of the eighteenth century and indicates that he, more fully and intensely than any of his contemporaries, anticipated the problematic vision of America that was to dominate the literary imagination of the nineteenth and twentieth centuries.

ST. JOHN DE CREVECOEUR

By **THOMAS PHILBRICK**

University of Pittsburgh

Twayne Publishers, Inc.   ::   New York

FOR MARIANNE

Preface

Thus one species of evil is balanced by another; thus the fury of one element is repressed by the power of the other. In the midst of this great, this astonishing equipoise Man struggles and lives.

AT THE CENTER of the vision to which St. John de Crèvecoeur's writings give expression is an extraordinary awareness of the opposing forces that clash and contend in the natural universe, in human societies, and within the individual consciousness. His own experience, which had schooled him in vicissitude and paradox, required him again and again to revise his attitudes, his way of life, and his very identity. In their great variety, all his writings reflect in one way or another those lessons in change and contradiction; all contribute to the delineation of that astonishing equipoise which he discovered reality to be.

If this book has an ax to grind, it is that Crèvecoeur's works are indeed informed by the awareness of thrust and counterthrust in nature and in man, and that the best of them are distinguished by the complex artistry which an adequate representation of that vision demands. Although I have tried to do justice to Crèvecouer's many claims upon our attention, I have stressed, perhaps inordinately, the nature and extent of his achievement as a literary artist. I have come to be persuaded that those values which earlier commentators have identified in Crèvecoeur's writings—the acuteness and historical importance of his analysis of American society, the charm of his descriptions of nature, and the vigor of his sketches of rural life—are subsumed under the larger aims and achievements of his art.

This book attempts, therefore, to trace the evolution of that art through all of Crèvecoeur's major writings, both in English and in French. In the interest of readers who may know little French, all quotations from *Lettres d'un Cultivateur Américain* and from *Voyage dans la Haute Pensylvanie et dans l'état de New-York* are in English translation except where the French prose style itself is a matter of concern. Unless otherwise indicated, translations from the French of Crèvecoeur and his commentators are my own.

Permission to quote extensively from copyrighted material has generously been granted by the following publishers: Columbia University Press for Julia P. Mitchell, *St. Jean de Crèvecoeur*; Yale University Press for Henri L. Bourdin, Ralph H. Gabriel, and Stanley T. Williams, eds., Crèvecoeur's *Sketches of Eighteenth Century America*; and the University of Michigan Press for Clarissa S. Bostelmann, translator, Crèvecoeur's *Journey into Northern Pennslyvania and the State of New York*.

My deep indebtedness to those who have written before on Crèvecoeur, particularly to Howard C. Rice for his thorough analysis of the content and impact of Crèvecoeur's thought and to Albert E. Stone, Jr., for his penetrating insights into the art of *Letters from an American Farmer*, will be obvious. I am grateful to the staffs of the University of Pittsburgh Library, the Harvard College Library, and the University of Vermont Library for their kind assistance in the preparation of this book.

THOMAS PHILBRICK

University of Pittsburgh
May, 1968

Contents

ABOUT THE AUTHOR

Thomas Philbrick was born in Providence, Rhode Island, in 1929. He received his A.B. in 1950 from Brown University and his M.A. in 1954 and his Ph.D. in 1959 from Harvard University. He has taught at Harvard, the University of Vermont, and Union College. At present he is a professor of English at the University of Pittsburgh.

His special interests are in American literature, particularly American romanticism and the early development of American fiction. He is the author of *James Fenimore Cooper and the Development of American Sea Fiction*, published by Harvard University Press in 1961, and the editor of Cooper's *The Crater*, published in the John Harvard Library series by Harvard University Press in 1962. He has contributed articles on Melville and on Cooper to *PMLA*, *American Literature*, and *Nineteenth-Century Fiction*.

Chronology

1735   Michel-Guillaume-Jean de Crèvecoeur born January 31 in Caen, Normandy.

1754   Travels to England where he resides with relations in Salisbury.

1755–   Sails for Canada. Enlists as a cadet in the colonial militia;
1759   serves as a surveyor and cartographer during the French and Indian War. Commissioned a lieutenant in the regular Regiment de la Sarre in 1758. Wounded in the battle of Quebec in September, 1759. Sells his commission in October.

1759–   Arrives in New York City on December 16, 1759. Adopts
1768   the name of James Hector St. John. Travels extensively in the wilderness of northern New York and Vermont as a surveyor and Indian trader. Farms rented land in New York. Becomes a naturalized citizen of New York on December 23, 1765. Tours the Atlantic seaboard in 1766 and the Ohio Valley and Great Lakes regions in 1767.

1769   Marries Mehitable Tippet on September 20. Buys 120 acres of land in Orange County, New York, in December. Begins writing essays and sketches on America.

1770   Names the new property Pine Hill and clears it for farming. Daughter America-Francès (Fanny) born on December 14.

1772   Son Guillaume-Alexandre (Ally) born on August 5.

1774   Makes a trip in the summer to the new settlements along the branches of the Susquehanna River. Son Philippe-Louis (Louis) born on October 22.

1775–   The Revolutionary War breaks out. The British occupy
1777   New York City in September, 1776. Orange County becomes a war zone, exposed to attack by Indian and Tory raiders.

1778   Applies early in the year to American authorities for permission to travel to France by way of New York City.

Visits in the summer the Wyoming Valley of Pennsylvania, devastated by an Indian attack on July 3.

1779   Arrives at New York City with his son Ally early in the year. Arrested by the British in July; imprisoned as a suspected American spy. Released under surveillance in October.

1780   Sails from New York on September 1; lands in Dublin in mid-October.

1781   Sells fifteen essays and sketches in London to the publishers Davis and Davies on May 20. Unknown to Crèvecoeur, Orange County is raided by Indians, Pine Hill is burned, his wife dies, and Fanny and Louis are taken in by a neighbor. Crèvecoeur reaches France on August 2; goes to Paris at the end of the year as a protégé of the Marquis de Turgot. Gustave Fellowes of Boston adopts Fanny and Louis but is unable to contact their father.

1782   *Letters from an American Farmer* is published in London early in the year. Crèvecoeur meets Madame d'Houdetot.

1783   Receives appointment as consul to New York, New Jersey, and Connecticut in June. Prepares a French version of the *Letters*. Arrives in New York on November 19; learns of the fate of his family.

1784   Undertakes his duties as consul; is reunited with his children in Boston. *Lettres d'un Cultivateur Américain* is published in Paris in December.

1785–   Returns to France on sick leave in July, 1785. Prepares an
1787   expanded version of the *Lettres,* published in Paris in April, 1787. Returns to New York in July.

1789   Elected to membership in the American Philosophical Society on January 16. The French Revolution begins.

1790   Fanny marries the French diplomat Otto in April. Crèvecoeur returns to France on furlough in June; retires to Normandy.

1792   Attempts to resign from the consular service. His appointment is revoked in December.

1793–   The Reign of Terror overtakes France. Ally escapes to
1794   Hamburg; Louis, to the United States. Crèvecoeur, living in obscurity and poverty, unsuccessfully attempts to go to America.

1795   The Directory takes control of France. Crèvecoeur joins
       Ally in Germany in May.
1796– Returns to France in April, 1796. Lives quietly in Nor-
1800   mandy with his father, who dies in 1799, the year that
       Bonaparte becomes First Consul. Crèvecoeur begins a
       new book on America.
1801   *Voyage dans la Haute Pensylvanie et dans l'état de New-
       York* is published in Paris.
1802– Visits Otto and Fanny in London in the summer of 1802.
1806   Returns to reside in Otto's country house at Lesches.
1806– Ally dies in July, 1806. Grief-stricken, Crèvecoeur joins
1809   Fanny in Munich where Otto is stationed as the French
       ambassador. Forced to return to France in April, 1809, by
       the advance of the Austrian army.
1809– Lives peacefully at Otto's house in Sarcelles. Dies of a
1813   heart ailment on November 12, 1813.

ST. JOHN DE CRÈVECOEUR

CHAPTER 1

The Man and His Masks

THE MOTORIST who travels east on Route 94 from Chester in Orange County, New York, may notice a historical marker on the left side of the road about three miles beyond the town. The sign, erected by the State Education Department in 1936, bears a brief inscription: "Pine Hill Farm. Hector St. John de Crèvecoeur, 1735–1813, settled here 1769 and here wrote 'Letters from an American Farmer' (London 1782)." Apart from the sign and a row of huge sycamores, perhaps five or six feet in diameter at their base, little distinguishes the site from the surrounding country, a region of lettuce fields and corn patches, of pastures for Holstein cattle and trotting horses. The house which is behind the sign and the sycamores is oddly shaped, it is true, as if an ordinary frame house together with its porch had been set atop an older brick structure. But the children playing on the lawn, the barking dogs, and the men tinkering with the engine of a worn-out car in the driveway might be seen anywhere in one of the remnants of rural landscape that still survive within the Eastern megalopolis.

Nothing but the massive sycamores suggests the aura of a deep past—suggests that two hundred years ago an obscure Frenchman who called himself Hector St. John had settled here with his new American wife, had drained and planted the flat fields across the road, and had dug the cellar and built the foundation on which this house stands. Nothing tells of the ten years he farmed his land and his mind, constructing at Pine Hill a microcosm of that best of all possible worlds which he hoped America might be. Nor does the present scene speak of the collapse of that hope amid the turmoil of revolution and the violence of guerrilla warfare, the cataclysm that destroyed the farm and transformed the American farmer into a servant of the court of Versailles. Nothing in the setting proclaims that here was played out the central episode in a life of astonishing vicissitude and that here was rooted the experience from which emerged some of the most subtle and engaging writing of eighteenth-century American literature.

I *Beginnings*

Michel-Guilliaume-Jean de Crèvecoeur was born in Caen on January 31, 1735, the son of Augustin de Crèvecoeur, a respectable if undistinguished member of the petty nobility of Normandy. The boy's mother was the daughter of a prosperous banker, who had given her a better education than that enjoyed by most women of the time. In the summer, the family lived on a country estate in Pierrepont, a village a few miles northeast of Caen. Winters were spent in Caen itself, the tedium being broken by an occasional week or more in Paris, where the boy's father renewed his ties with the fashionable world of the court. Crèvecouer's childhood was an uneventful one, firmly guided by his father's grave and autocratic rule.

The Jesuit Collège du Mont in Caen, to which the boy was sent for his schooling, offered no relief from the austere regime of his father. "If only you knew," Crèvecoeur later wrote to his own children, "in what a filthy dormitory, in what a dark and chilly garret I was confined at your age and with what severity I was treated, how they fed me and clothed me!"[1] But, if his school supplied little beauty or excitement, the ancient furnishings of the family home and the medieval architecture of its neighborhood exerted a strong pull on his imagination. In old age he recalled that "from my earliest youth I had a passion for pondering every trace of antiquity which I came across—worm-eaten furniture, tapestries, old family portraits, and the Gothic parchments of the fifteenth and sixteenth centuries that I tried to decipher held an indefinable charm for me. When I was older, I loved to stroll in the solitude of graveyards, to examine the tombstones, and to make out the moss-grown epitaphs."[2]

Such exercises of the romantic imagination as these would seem to have been the young Crèvecoeur's chief avenue of escape from the dreary routine of home and school before 1754. In that year, possibly because of a quarrel with his father, he was sent to England, where he lived in Salisbury with two aged maiden ladies named Mutel, distant relations of the family. There he learned the language, presumably completed his education, and fell in love. But the girl, the only daughter of a businessman, died before they could marry; and the next year Crèvecoeur embarked for America, arriving in Canada at the outset of the French and Indian War.

He immediately enlisted in the Canadian militia and, applying the mathematical ability that he had demonstrated in school at Caen, served the French forces as a surveyor and cartographer. In this service he gained a direct acquaintance with the American wilderness and the American Indian, for his duties took him far into the region of the Ottawa River northwest of Montreal and, in the summer of 1757, to Fort William Henry on Lake George, where he witnessed the surrender of the fort to Montcalm and the massacre of the defeated garrison by the Indian allies of the French. In 1758 Crèvecoeur was recommended by Baron de Breteuil and the Marquis d'Houdetot, two influential friends of his father, for a commission as second lieutenant in the Regiment de la Sarre, a unit of the regular French army. In 1759 a plan that he had drawn of Fort William Henry was presented to the king, and the young officer was cited for his courage and ability in the *Gazette de France.*

In the fall of that year, however, Crèvecoeur's promising military career came to an abrupt and, it would seem, ignominious end. Wounded in the defense of Quebec against Wolfe's army, he was hospitalized in that city after the French capitulation. In the official correspondence that deals with the repatriation of the officers of the Regiment de la Sarre, there is speculation whether the "others" would want Crèvecoeur to return to France with them. Never in later life did Crèvecoeur refer to his army service in Canada. The nature of his disgrace, if indeed it was a disgrace, will probably remain a mystery.[3] All that is certain is that his fellow officers required him to resign from the regiment, that he sold his commission in October, and that on December 16, 1759, he arrived in New York City on board a British military transport vessel.

II   *The Creation of Hector St. John*

Crèvecoeur's activities during the next few years are particularly difficult to trace, for these were the years in which he deliberately buried one identity and shaped a new one. Lieutenant Michel Jean de Crèvecoeur, scion of the Norman aristocracy and officer in His Most Christian Majesty's army, vanishes, and in his place appears J. Hector St. John, itinerant surveyor and merchant. Fitted for the wilderness by his military experience, he traveled extensively through British North America, surveying the new country and trading with the Indians. In 1764 he explored the region which was to become Vermont and was adopted by the Oneidas of northern New York as Cahio-Harra. In 1766 he toured the Atlantic colonies from New Hampshire to Virginia and then, in the next year, plunged inland on an excursion of six months to the Ohio Valley and the Great Lakes.

Surely this period of wandering was as much a time of self-exploration as it was of physical travel and discovery. Released from the conventions and proscriptions of his family and the army, he threw himself into a life of ranging experience, widening his responses and testing his capacities. But it was not all wandering. In the intervals between his trips, he farmed rented land in the Hudson Valley, trying out a role which constituted still another departure from his life before 1759. In 1765 he met Mehitable Tippet of Westchester, the daughter of a substantial landowner; and in that same year he became a naturalized citizen of New York. On September 20, 1769, he married Miss Tippet and, three months later, bought one hundred and twenty acres of uncleared land in Orange County. There he set about perfecting the identity by which the world was to come to know him, that of the American farmer.

Crèvecoeur was well prepared for his new life. By this time he was indeed an American, thoroughly acquainted with the language and customs of the new country. More than most native Americans, he knew firsthand the extent and diversity of the British colonies, from the cities of the coast to the wilderness of the interior. He had become a student of the process of settlement, following with eager interest the techniques by which the forest was cleared, the farms planted, and new communities formed. He knew his own property well, for as early as 1764 he had farmed the Cromline meadows adjacent to his newly acquired acres.

With the aid of his new wife and his neighbors, the thirty-five-year-old soldier, surveyor, and salesman set about the formidable task of converting the raw land that he had bought into a homestead. Early in 1770 he felled the first tree at "Pine Hill," as he called his farm. During the next few years he built a house, a neat frame structure of two stories which replaced the log cabin that was his first shelter, drained the swamp across the road, and planted an orchard on the hillside. On December 14, 1770, his first child was born, a girl whose name, America-Francès, was an emblem of her father's career. Two boys—Guillaume-Alexandre, born in 1772, and Phillipe-Louis, born in 1774—completed the family.

Rigorous though the work was, Crèvecoeur's life at Pine Hill was not cramped by the unrelieved physical labor and isolation which most pioneer farmers endured. By 1770, Orange County was no longer a new country, for the road which divided Crèvecoeur's property was a principal route to New Jersey. Greycourt Inn, a short distance from Pine Hill, had long served travelers, and the village of Chester was only three miles down the road. Crèvecoeur's circle of acquaintances soon included most of the established men of the county—freeholders like himself, the proprietors of ironworks and mills, and local officials like Jesse Woodhull, the sheriff of Orange County.

Indeed, his connections ranged far beyond the county limits. He was a frequent visitor at Coldengham, the manorial seat of Cadwallader Colden some twenty miles from Pine Hill; and there he enjoyed the conversation of the guests who were attracted to the home of the scientist, historian of the Iroquois Confederacy, and lieutenant-governor of New York; there, too, he had access to an excellent library, well stocked with the latest European publications. His two closest friends resided in New York City; the clergyman who had performed his marriage and baptized his children, the Reverend Tétard, and the merchant William Seton, both widely traveled and well-educated men whose horizons extended far beyond the borders of their province.

Crèvecoeur's life at Pine Hill, then, was neither one of back-woods isolation nor one of rural retirement. He was in steady contact with some of the best minds in the colony, in touch not only with husking bees and barn-raisings but with English political debate and French social theorizing. He had enough money to support himself in a degree of grace and leisure. A watercolor of Pine Hill, which he painted in 1778, shows in the distance his attractive house surrounded by his broad fields and orchards, his Negro hand plowing in the foreground, and he and his wife relaxing in the shade of a nearby tree.[4]

He had the time to make extensive trips in 1774 and 1776 into the new territory along the branches of the Susquehanna. And he had time for writing. About 1769 he began composing a series of short sketches and essays on the New World, drawing on the observations that he had made in the course of his travels, on information furnished by his friends and his reading, and on his own experience as an American farmer at Pine Hill.

"I am no author," Crèvecoeur wrote to a friend in 1785, "but a plain scribbler, who has compiled a good many sheets, he hardly knows how."[5] The habit of scribbling was probably firmly established before he began to write at Pine Hill. In childhood he may have written down his romantic responses to the antiquities of Caen.[6] As a surveyor and cartographer, he must have kept a journal and developed the practice of accurately and systematically recording the observations that he made on his travels. Now enjoying the stability of his life as a farmer and stimulated by the interest and encouragement of his friends, Crèvecoeur began to write seriously and regularly. The earliest of his writings at Pine Hill, those which were composed before 1774, consist chiefly of impressionistic travel sketches that center on such varied locales as Lisbon, the islands of Jamaica, Bermuda, Nantucket, and Martha's Vineyard, and the colonies of Virginia and South Carolina. Some of the sketches are clearly the outgrowth of his journeys before 1769; others seem to derive from his reading and the reports of his acquaintances. Dealing with subjects much closer to his own immediate experience, the writings of the period between 1774 and 1776 are comprised of general essays on American manners and attitudes and of intimate accounts of the experiences and techniques of the American farmer. The last group of sketches, written in 1777 and 1778, describes the devastating impact of the Revolutionary War upon American life.

In all, three substantial volumes of manuscripts survive from the years during which Crèvecoeur wrote at Pine Hill, manuscripts from which were drawn nearly the entire contents of the two published volumes of his English writings and the nucleus of the two editions of *Lettres d'un Cultivateur Américain.* The scope and intensity of the twenty-eight manuscript sketches suggest that writing was no incidental occupation for Crèvecoeur at Pine Hill, a gentlemanly diversion from the labors of agriculture, but a major object of his energies and increasingly the center of his interest.

The European who settles in America, wrote Crèvecoeur at Pine Hill, undergoes a "great metamorphosis," "a sort of resurrection" by which he is transformed into a new man (*Letters,* 75, 73). The context of the remark is a general discussion of the conversion of the European peasant into the American freeholder, but the words apply with a special force to his own experience. For Hector St. John, the farmer of Pine Hill and commentator on America and its society, was in an extraordinarily literal sense a new man, a man divorced from his past and his inheritance—a man whose language, religion, political outlook, and occupation were rooted in the New World to which he had come. The citizen of New York, the loyal adherent of the British crown, had replaced altogether the young Norman who had sailed for Canada in 1755. By 1772 he had severed his ties to France so completely that his father, uncertain whether Crèvecoeur was alive or dead and puzzling over how the inheritance should be arranged, appealed to the British government for aid in the search:

> The object of this inquiry is named Michel Guillaume Jean de Crèvecoeur; he is a gentleman born in Caen, capital of lower Normandy; he is nearly thirty-eight years old. His height is five feet four inches—he has a very handsome appearance, is sturdy and well proportioned.
>
> He has reddish-brown hair and used to wear a wig, his face is a little long but nevertheless full, his skin is fair but freckled; his eyes are clear and brown, his eyebrows are brown also and thick; his forehead is handsome and open, his nose a little long; his freckles are small and resemble bits of bran; they extend to his

hands, which are covered with them; his hands are rather large and lanky.

An expatriot for eighteen years, he lived in England for ten or eleven years; he first referred himself to the Misses Mutel, elderly maidens in their seventies who lived in the town of Salisbury. Through these ladies, he came in contact with certain individuals having business establishments in Philadelphia and in Pennsylvania, and he lived in that province of New England in the city of Philadelphia for eight or nine years. He held the post of associate or agent of a businessman whose name and branch of commerce are not known, and the last news received from him came in the year 1767. He must know English perfectly, at least he passes himself off as an Englishman. It is not known if he is married, or if he has been; it is known only that shortly after his arrival in England he became engaged to the only daughter of a merchant, that she died before they could be married, and that this episode procured him the interests which he had in Philadelphia.[7]

The inquiry makes it clear that Crèvecoeur's parents were aware of his efforts to conceal his military service in Canada—a secret so important, it would seem, that, even in the urgency of their attempt to find him, they still maintained the fiction of the extended residence in England by which Hector St. John accounted for his past. The document suggests, too, that Crèvecoeur had so fully embraced his new identity and so completely buried his old one that he had renounced any intention of returning to France to claim his inheritance. The author of the *Letters* was indeed no foreign observer, no sojourner from Europe who viewed the life of the New World as a detached spectacle. His book was written from the inside, by a man wholly committed to the life that it describes.

By 1775, then, the transformation of Michel-Guillaume-Jean de Crèvecoeur into Hector St. John was complete. His own future and that of his offspring were to be lived by the terms of his new identity. The children were given a Protestant baptism and prepared for a life on an American farm, for Pine Hill, not a Norman estate, was to be their legacy. The farm flourished, the writing progressed; it must have seemed to Crèvecoeur as if his own experience abundantly confirmed the bright image of America that he was sketching in his manuscripts. And then, suddenly and catastrophically, everything changed.

III *The Collapse of a World*

If Crèvecoeur's writings before 1776 are remarkable for their almost total lack of reference to the burgeoning controversy between the colonies and England, those composed after that date are utterly devoted to it. It would seem that Crèvecoeur, secure and prosperous on his farm, intent on the happy future that his children were to enjoy, and blinded, perhaps, by the bland confidence of the Tory circles that he frequented, ignored every indication of the growing violence of the dispute and of the threat that it posed to the ordered tranquility that he so delighted in contemplating. When the fighting broke out in Massachusetts in 1775 and swiftly spread to the other colonies, his response was one of shock and despair.

Pine Hill offered no refuge from the war. Only a day's march from New York City, the seat of British power in North America from 1776 until the end of the war, and yet far enough inland to be exposed to the raids of Tory partisans and their Indian allies, Orange County soon became a critical war zone. Within a few miles of Pine Hill were a large camp for prisoners-of-war, an important powder mill, and the foundry which forged much of the chain that the Americans rigged across the Hudson River at West Point, fifteen miles to the east, in an effort to prevent Sir Henry Clinton's forces at New York City from ravaging the Hudson Valley, as they had done in the fall of 1777. West and north of Orange County, Loyalist guerrillas under John Butler and Indian war parties led by Joseph Brant terrorized the frontier, destroying the settlements at Wyoming and Cherry Valley in 1778. But Clinton, Butler, and Brant were not the only threats to the happiness of life at Pine Hill. A more immediate danger sprang from the corrosive atmosphere of enmity and suspicion which the war engendered among the inhabitants of the county.

For Crèvecoeur, the conflict was not a war for independence, a struggle against an external enemy, but a civil war and a social revolution, a war that pitted neighbor against neighbor and shattered the structure of society. He shared the Tory sympathies of his wife's family and of friends like William Seton, but his loyalty to the cause of Britain was overshadowed by his revulsion from the turmoil and suffering of the war itself. The only real virtue of British rule was that it had permitted the kind of life that he had constructed at Pine Hill. Orange County was now governed by a revolutionary Committee of Public Safety, a body of men who were quick to smell treason and eager to taste the flavor of power. Ridiculous though these upstarts often appeared because of their awkward exercise of their new authority, that authority was real enough. They could require citizens to take an oath of loyalty to the new revolutionary government and punish non-compliance by exile and the expropriation of property. Their justice was crude and fanatic; feeding on rumors, it was quick and arbitrary in execution.

That Crèvecoeur himself suffered persecution at the hands of the commissioners of Orange County is unlikely. He must have taken the oath of loyalty, for his property remained his until he sold it long after the war. It would seem that his bitter contempt for the revolutionary government and his abhorrence of the war itself were confined chiefly to his manuscripts, for the whole pacific temper of the man argues against any overt resistance. After the war, he renewed his ties with his friends in Orange County, apparently without any risk of embarrassment because of his conduct during the war. Undoubtedly Crèvecoeur was known for his lack of enthusiasm for the Patriot cause, and perhaps his habit of writing and his skill in making maps aroused some suspicion; but he was not harried out of the county as a Tory.

Nevertheless, early in 1778, Crèvecoeur applied for official permission to go to British-occupied New York City, there to embark for Europe. The reasons for his decision to abandon his wife and his two youngest children to the hazards of Orange County are obscure. The ostensible purpose of the journey was to establish the place of his children in the line of succession to the Norman rank and property of his father, a task of some difficulty; for, according to legal record, they had been born to an American farmer named St. John, not to the heir of Augustin de Crèvecoeur. Ally, his firstborn son, was to accompany him as living proof of his claims.

Although there is evidence that Crèvecoeur had long entertained the notion of making a trip to Europe,[8] one wonders why he waited until this moment of maximum danger to undertake the long and uncertain journey, one which required him to cross the American lines into New York City, arrange passage to England, and make his way to France, newly become the ally of the Patriots and the enemy of England. Perhaps now, when his dream of America had become a nightmare, when the society on which he had placed his hopes for his children's future and his own seemed to be collapsing in chaos, he turned with a species of desperation to the radical alternative, the Old World, as the locus of stability and order. The matter of the inheritance—the good father's concern for his children's financial security—was the conscious reason for the decision. But in the timing of the journey and in its hit-or-miss execution, one senses an undertone of panic, as if it were the kind of impulsive flight from trouble that seems to have played a part twenty years before in his separation from the French army in Canada.

Some of Crèvecoeur's neighbors in Orange County imagined still other motives for the journey. One local official reported to Governor Clinton that "the people of our country are much alarmed at their apprehensions of St. John's being permitted to go to New York. I asked one of the most sensible of them what damage he could Doe; he observed that he might Advise the burning of Sterling [iron] works in order to prevent our giting the Chain done. I told him I believed you would Consider well the matter Before you would grant that permission."[9] At last, however, under rigid conditions laid down by General McDougall, commander of the American forces at Fishkill, Crèvecoeur was granted permission to travel by land along the west bank of the Hudson to the British lines. Early in 1779, with the six-year-old Ally at his side, he made his way into New York City.

Once there, Crèvecoeur found himself obliged to devise a new identity, that of the victim of rebel persecution. The rations for which he applied to the inspector of refugee claims would be "the only reward of 4 years of Contumely Receiv'd, of Fines Imposed, Emprisonments," and the other miseries that he had suffered by reason of his loyalty to the Crown.[10] The latest revision of the history of Hector St. John was submitted to the British officials who interrogated Crèvecoeur:

The account Mr. St. John gives of himself is that he is a native of Caen in Normandy, but came into this Country many years ago and was naturalized; that he first went into the Mercantile Line, but afterwards bought a farm in Orange County, on which he Settled, but was obliged to quit it about Six Months Ago, to leave his family & property behind, on Account of the Persecution he underwent from his attachment to Government, & that during his leisure hours he amused himself with making such literary Observations as occur'd to him, but which he is convinced will upon Perusal, do him Credit in the opinion of those attached to the King's Government, that he has never kept them secret from those of his Acquaintance who were thus Attached, but took pains & found great Difficulty, whilst among the Rebels, to conceal them. . . .[11]

Crèvecoeur had those "literary Observations" with him in New York in a small trunk. Whether he brought them along only as evidence of his loyalty or whether he had some vague hope of finding a publisher for them is uncertain, but the contents of the trunk, the manuscripts of the essays and sketches that he had written at Pine Hill, represented the only fruit of his ten years of work on the farm. Nearly penniless, he and Ally depended for their subsistence on the rations which they received from the refugee office and on the assistance which Tory friends in the city could give them. Some small surveying jobs earned him a little money during the first few months in New York while he and Ally waited for the chance to embark for Great Britain.

In the summer of 1779, all of Crèvecoeur's efforts to protect himself in New York by merging with the Tory refugees who thronged the city were frustrated by an ironic turn of events. If he himself had overstated his activities and sufferings on behalf of the crown, an anonymous informant now furnished the British authorities with a still more distorted report of his activities on the side of the Patriots. St. John, the accuser charged, was guilty of corresponding with Washington, of having made a map of New York Harbor, and of having persuaded a neighbor to take the oath of allegiance to the revolutionary government of his state. All three allegations probably contained a measure of truth, but their import was hardly threatening. Nevertheless, they were enough to persuade the British, made doubly suspicious by Crèvecoeur's French origin, to arrest him and to imprison him for three months in a jail for political suspects and prisoners-of-war.

Living amidst filth and disease, ignorant of the sentence that he might ultimately receive, anxious for the safety of his wife and children and powerless to aid them, Crèvecoeur was reduced to desperation. When he learned that Ally, who was staying with friends on Long Island, was critically ill with a fever, he suffered a nervous collapse. By early October, 1779, when William Seton was able to procure his release on bond, Crèvecoeur was a shattered man, physically ill and in a state of psychic shock. Somehow, he managed to survive the winter of 1779-80 by finding employment helping a party of British soldiers break up the hulks of abandoned ships; his pay was firewood.

At last, late in the summer of 1780, the chance for escape came. On September 1, Crèvecoeur and his little boy sailed in a large convoy bound for the British Isles. Landing in Ireland after a passage of six weeks, he left Ally in Dublin and went on to London, where he sought a publisher for his manuscripts. He had the good fortune to make contact with the bookseller Thomas Davies, an acquaintance of Samuel Johnson and "a friendly and very hospitable man," Boswell assures his reader.[12] Perhaps Crèvecoeur found him so, for on May 20 he contracted to sell the first volume of his manuscripts to the firm of Davies and Davis for thirty guineas, "with promise of a present if the public likes the book,"[13] and with the understanding that a second volume would be published if the first were well received.

IV *Who Is Crèvecoeur?*

Retrieving Ally, Crèvecoeur crossed the Channel and, on August 2, touched the soil of France for the first time in twenty-seven years. His initial destination was his father's summer residence at Pierrepont. The matter of the inheritance, the great object of his journey, was not to be soon settled; three years later he was still enmeshed in the effort to establish the legal identity and legitimacy of his children. For the present, his chief task was to make a place for himself in French society and to prepare the way for his return to America and the recovery of his family and property. To accomplish that task, his father enlisted the aid of an old and influential friend, Madame d'Houdetot, a fifty-year-old leader of Parisian society whose celebrated charm had won her the love of Rousseau and Saint-Lambert.

Within a few days of Crèvecoeur's arrival in France, Madame d'Houdetot wrote to her good friend Benjamin Franklin, then in France on his wartime diplomatic mission, recommending to him "a young American. . . . He is a Frenchman by birth, but for a long time has been established in your country, under the protection of your laws, to which he is faithful. He has come here to see his family after having lost the greater part of his possessions through the present war. His name is Crèvecoeur, and he is the son of a friend, of more than twenty years' standing, of my husband and myself."[14] Madame d'Houdetot's letter indicates the shape of the new identity which Crèvecoeur was contriving for himself in France. He was still the victim of war, but now he was a firm supporter of the Patriot cause, a figure that united in a single character all those qualities which most appealed to the French imagination of the 1780's. He was an inhabitant of that New World in which French interest had been stirred by the recent alliance with the United States; he was a Patriot, an adherent of those wise and humane principles of the *philosophes* which French liberals believed that the Americans were putting into practice; and he was a sufferer at the hands of Britain, a victim to whom both the sentimental and the patriotic could respond.

A chance encounter on the coast of Normandy soon gave Crèvecoeur an opportunity to establish himself in his new role. In late August, he met five American seamen who had just landed in France after escaping from a British prison. Taking the men to his father's house, he fed and clothed them and helped them secure a passage back to America; in return for his kindness, they promised to ask Gustave Fellowes, a prominent citizen of Boston and the kinsman of their leader, to obtain news of Crèvecoeur's family in Orange County, from whom he had received no word for nearly a year. On August 28, Crèvecoeur himself wrote to Franklin describing his efforts on behalf of the seamen and offering his services as an official American agent for escaped prisoners-of-war: ". . . if from the Information you might receive of me from the Count de Houdetot you thought me capable of discharging this office I'd readily accept of it without either fee or Reward, glad on the contrary as a good Frenchman and a good American to contribute my Mite towards the Success of this grand, this useful revolution—Excuse this Letter, it is zeal and the purest zeal which hath dictated it."[15]

Since the zealous Patriot signed his letter "St. John," Franklin was in doubt whether he was the same person as the Crèvecoeur whom Madame d'Houdetot had recommended to him. But soon both she and Crèvecoeur wrote to clear up the confusion; the latter explained that "I am so great a Stranger to the manners of this, tho' my native Country (having quitted it very young) that I Never dreamt I had any other, than the old family name [of St. Jean]—I was greatly astonished when at my late return, I saw myself under the Necessity of being Called by that of Crèvecoeur."[16] He had momentarily entangled himself in his own web of concealment. Surely he had not forgotten his own full name, but he was still reluctant to use it, even though more than twenty years had passed since it had been dropped from the roll of the Regiment de la Sarre. Madame d'Houdetot again sounded the main theme: "I know," she assured Franklin, "that he is very much attached to the United States and that no one has felt more than he the calamities attendant upon the present war."[17] In December Crèvecoeur once more wrote to Franklin, this time to congratulate him on Washington's great victory at Yorktown, an event that "must necessarily convulse with joy the hearts of every loyal American as well as those of every good Frenchman."[18]

That Crèvecoeur's own inmost heart was convulsed with joy by the American triumph is doubtful, but clearly the only course open to him was to proclaim his fervent support of the Revolution. The Tory cause was by now lost, and any hope of a return to America would depend on his coming as a firm friend of the new republic. If strategic considerations like this one demanded the new stance, it is not likely that his real sympathies opposed them. The months of anxiety and hardship in New York City had dampened his admiration of the mildness and stability of British rule in America, and it is hard to believe that in France he returned to the attitudes and opinions he had held at Pine Hill. Yet it would be a mistake to accept Crèvecoeur's portrait of himself as the ardent Patriot at face value. If his experiences since he had left Pine Hill had taught him anything, they had strengthened his old distrust of parties and causes.

Having established a line of communication with Franklin, Crèvecoeur now began to widen his acquaintance in the society of his native country. The Marquis de Turgot, a distant relation of the family and brother of the famous minister of the king, took Crèvecoeur to Paris at the end of the year and introduced him to the upper echelons of French social and intellectual life, a program that included visits twice a week to the home of the great naturalist Buffon. Soon after his arrival in Paris, Madame d'Houdetot sent her young American, whom she had not yet met, an invitation; but Crèvecoeur, in a fit of shyness, put her off by pleading illness until her insistence made further delay blatantly discourteous. In March, 1782, the two met. Madame d'Houdetot, charmed by Crèvecoeur's Anglo-French speech and manners, his exotic history, and his diffidence, at once took him under her wing. She invited him to reside in her mansion in Paris, led him to the art galleries and libraries, and acquainted him with the members of the brilliant circle that she had drawn around her, aristocrats like La Rochefoucauld-Liancourt and the Princess de Beauvau and artists and intellectuals like Jean le Rond d'Alembert, Guy-Jean-Baptiste Target, Jean-François de Saint-Lambert, Friedrich-Melchior Grimm, and Jean-François de La Harpe. "How that lady welcomed me!" he wrote years later, "how promptly she understood me, reassured me! How skifully by her perseverance and her little unobtrusive compliments she made me over into a new man! What rapid progress in the knowledge of French, in the usages of the world, etc., my desire to merit the esteem of this new friend made me accomplish!"[19]

Meanwhile, in early 1782, Davies and Davis published *Letters from an American Farmer* in London. The book, an immediate success, attracted wide and favorable notice in the British reviews. Although the *Letters* soon went through a second English edition and was published in Ireland, Holland, and Germany, it was known to few in France beyond Madame d'Houdetot's circle. At the urging of his patroness and her friend the Princess de Beauvau, Crèvecoeur undertook the preparation of a French edition. The labor of translation and expansion was arduous, for his French was still rusty. By early 1783 the work was nearly done, and one of his new acquaintances, the critic Pierre-Louis Lacretelle, published an excerpt from the book and an account of its author in the *Mercure de France* in January. The announcement proved to be premature, however, for a few months later the manuscript was stolen and a new one was not finished until July.

If his efforts to establish a literary reputation in France were meeting with frustration and delay, Crèvecoeur enjoyed a brilliant, unexpected success in a far different quarter. In the spring of 1783, while the peace treaty between the United States and Great Britain was under negotiation at Versailles and France was preparing the diplomatic machinery for conducting its relations with the new nation, Madame d'Houdetot managed to secure for her protégé a commission to write an elaborate report on the United States for de Castries, the minister in charge of the diplomatic service. Installed in the d'Houdetot apartment at Versailles, Crèvecoeur worked for seven weeks on the document. The government was delighted by the result and rewarded the writer by putting his name at the head of the list of sixteen competitors for the consular posts to be established in America. Crèvecoeur received his formal appointment as consul to New York, Connecticut, and New Jersey, his first choice, in early July, and, basking in the congratulations of the court, he returned to Caen to prepare for his departure.

V Return to America

Although the manuscript of the French version of the *Letters* was now ready for publication, the governmental censors were slow in granting their approval, and Crèvecoeur was forced to ask his friends Saint-Lambert, Target, and Lacretelle to see the book through the press. In mid-September he embarked for America on board one of the ships of the new French packet line that he had helped to establish while he was at Versailles. On November 19, he landed in New York, where he was met at the dock by William Seton. With his return to America, Crèvecoeur was thrust once again into a world of confusion and turmoil. The city was in a precarious state, for these were the last few days of the British occupation. The harbor was clogged with the convoys that were to evacuate the remaining troops and those Loyalist families that had not already left for Nova Scotia and the mother country. Washington's army was poised on Harlem Heights, its leaders anxious to avoid contact with the British forces and yet concerned that rioting and looting might break out in the city before they could replace the royal authority with their own. The shabby streets and buildings, neglected during the years of the occupation, provided an appropriately somber setting for the news that Seton had to tell. Crèvecoeur's farm at Pine Hill had been burned in an Indian raid, his wife was dead, and his children had been carried off by a stranger, no one knew where.

Overcome with grief and worry, Crèvecoeur was too ill to attend the banquet in honor of Washington's entrance into the city on November 25. But early in December the dreadful uncertainty came to an end. Among the papers left by the British in the New York post office was a letter which Gustave Fellowes of Boston had written to him two years earlier. In it Fellowes told of receiving the letters and money which Crèvecoeur had attempted to send to his wife by way of the American seamen whom he had helped on the coast of Normandy. Deciding to look into the matter himself, Fellowes promptly set out from Boston for Orange County in spite of the winter and the war. There he found Fanny and Louis in the keeping of a family in Chester. Learning that the war-torn county could afford them neither schooling nor adequate food and clothing, Fellowes bundled up the children in his sleigh and took them back to Boston, where, his letter said, he intended to care for them as his own.

Although Crèvecoeur was at last in touch with his children, for the moment he was unable to join them in Boston. His consular duties were demanding and unfamiliar, and they were made all the more difficult by the nervous exhaustion from which he still suffered. And soon the most severe winter in fifty years set in, blocking for months all travel between New York and New England. Finally, in early April, he reached Boston and, searching out Fellowes' house, found his children safe and happy.

Crèvecoeur stayed in Boston with his children until the middle of June, when he returned to his consular duties in New York. Louis was sent to join Ally in Caen, but Fanny was to remain with the Fellowes family in Boston. With his personal affairs re-

solved, Crèvecoeur could now give his full energies to the task
for which he had beeen sent to America: solidifying the friendly
relations between the United States and France that their wartime alliance had brought into being. For the accomplishment of
that difficult assignment, he possessed a number of advantages,
not the least of which was the attractiveness of his personality.
An American who met this "very amiable Frenchman" in 1787
was delighted to find that he was to share his company on a trans-
atlantic passage: "Saint-John was by nature, by education, by his
writings and by his reputation a philanthropist. The milk of human kindness circulated in every vein. Mild, unassuming, prompt
to serve, slow to censure, extremely intelligent and universally
respected and beloved, his society on shipboard could not but be
a treasure."[20]

But the consul was not only a well-intentioned man; he was
also an informed one. Trained in early manhood as a scout and
surveyor, experienced in commerce and agriculture, and a lifelong
student of technological innovations, Crèvecoeur was admirably
equipped for his official role as observer and interpreter of America and its culture. Perhaps better than any other agent of the
French government, moreover, he knew the American ground,
knew its geography, its people, and their needs and values. The
force of these advantages is evinced by the range and energy of
Crèvecoeur's consular activities. Throughout his term of office he
was concerned with the packet service which his proposals had
helped to establish and which, for a time, he superintended. In
the interests of that service and of the French merchant marine
in general, he closely followed American developments in naval
architecture and the use of steam for marine propulsion. He interested himself deeply in the exchange of agricultural and botanical information between the two countries by helping to found
several botanical gardens in the United States, by writing a series
of articles on agricultural subjects for American newspapers, and
by promoting the use of alfalfa in America and of the locust tree
and potato in Europe. He struggled mightily to improve commercial relations between the two countries, informing French
merchants of the requirements of the American market and seeking the establishment of a free port for American goods in France.
Though his own religious attitudes were Deistic, he took an active

part in the founding of the first Catholic church in New York, St. Peter's, begun in 1786.

These services, and others like them, won Crèvecoeur the esteem and affection of the new republic. He was made an honorary citizen of several cities and elected to membership in a number of prominent organizations, among them the American Philosophical Society. His friend Ethan Allen went so far as to persuade the Vermont legislature to name the town of St. Johnsbury after him. But, despite these tokens of his success, Crèvecoeur's term as consul was not a particularly happy period of his life. Perhaps he felt torn between two worlds, the American one to which he was now only an official emissary and the French one, the world from which he received his employment and toward which he looked for his own advancement and that of his sons. To the government officials who employed him, he was not French enough; he was too like the Americans in his manner and attitudes, too fond of Anglo-Saxon laws and usages.[21] Increasingly, he was subject to long intervals of depression, in the depth of one of which he requested leave to return to France for rest and medical attention. In April, 1785, the furlough was granted, and Crèvecoeur immediately took a step that revealed the direction in which he was now traveling: in May he sold his property at Pine Hill. Having severed this last link with his old life, he embarked for France, there to renew the identity he had begun to shape four years before.

Ironically, Crèvecoeur, who was no longer an American in any meaningful sense, returned to France to find himself celebrated as the *Cultivateur Américain,* the representative of and spokesman for the whole pastoral and humanitarian dream which France had shaped around the idea of America. His two-volume translation and expansion of the *Letters,* which had been published in Paris at the end of 1784, had quickly established him as the authoritative interpreter of the New World to the Old. After spending the summer with his sons in Caen and the fall with Madame d'Houdetot at her country estate at Sannois, Crèvecoeur went to Paris to taste the sweetness of his new celebrity.

Once again came the round of visiting, of opera-going, and now he could attend a meeting of the French Academy, where he was gratified by the flattering attention that was paid him. It was a pleasant life indeed. Madame d'Houdetot played *maman* to Louis and Ally and saw to it that they were enrolled in the school in Paris which her own grandson attended. The Royal Agricultural Society of Paris honored the American Farmer by electing him to its membership. Clearly, a second edition of *Lettres d'un Culti-vateur Américain* was called for; and Crèvecoeur, determined to make it a grand production, set about the preparation of a third volume and the assembling of engraved illustrations and elaborate maps.

Having enjoyed the friendly reception that the new edition met on its publication in April, 1787, Crèvecoeur sailed for America to resume his consular duties. His second tour of duty was to involve him in new anxieties. Aboard the ship in which he returned to the United States was the Marquis de Lotbinière, who recognized the consul as an old companion-in-arms in Canada during the French and Indian war. That Crèvecoeur was disturbed by the chance encounter is suggested by Brissot de Warville, who visited him in America in 1788 and found him worried about the revelation of some secret: "Crèvecoeur, astounded by his prodigious success in France, feared that the mystery might be exposed and that he might be discharged from a post to which he was strongly attached."[22]

Brissot thought that Crèvecoeur's secret concerned his Loyalist sympathies during the Revolution, but it seems more likely that his fears of exposure related to this new and direct threat to his long concealment of his Canadian experience, for, if that experience involved some official disgrace, its disclosure might well cost him his post. There were other sources of uneasiness as well. Marshal de Castries had been dismissed as head of the consular service in the summer of 1787, and Crèvecoeur never felt that he enjoyed the full confidence of the new administration of La Luzerne. And in 1789 the confusing shifts of power of the French Revolution began. The one bright spot was Fanny's marriage in April, 1790, to Louis Guillaume Otto, secretary of the French legation to America and a diplomat of extraordinary promise. In May, having requested another leave of absence, Crèvecoeur sailed for France, never to return to America.

VI *The Last Decades*

The remaining twenty-three years of Crèvecoeur's life repeated the basic pattern of his experience—the quest for tranquillity and order in a world filled with violence and chaos. On the surface, his future appeared secure, even brilliant, upon his arrival in France in the summer of 1790. The Revolution was still in its relatively peaceful early stages. The Constitutionalists were in power for the moment, and the National Assembly was hard at work legislating into being the kind of state—liberal, enlightened, stable—which Crèvecoeur had always advocated. His friends and their friends—men like Lafayette, Brissot, and Target—occupied positions of power and influence; the time seemed ripe for him to advance to a post more important than that of consul to three states of the young republic across the Atlantic. As soon as he reached France, however, he bypassed Paris, the center of power and the source of promotion; recalling his two sons from school, he hastened with them to his father's house in Normandy, there to live in a studied obscurity. He was fifty-five years old, weary of public life, in ill-health, and far from sanguine about the benefits of revolutions.

In February, 1792, after the fall of Lafayette, the new minister of the diplomatic service, Bertrand de Molleville, ordered Crèvecoeur to return to his post. It was impossible, the consul replied; he had been ill with a fever for three weeks and was physically unable to obey. He submitted his resignation that month, but it was not acted upon until the end of the year; then his appointment, along with those of all other diplomatic representatives to the United States, was revoked. A quarrel with his father made it impossible for him to remain in Normandy, and he moved to Paris where, unable to get a pension from the government, he lived as cheaply and inconspicuously as he could.

With the outbreak of the Terror in 1793, the shelter in French society which Crèvecoeur had carefully constructed for himself gave way entirely. Nearly all of his powerful friends and guardians were guillotined or driven into exile. Otto's position in the government supplied a measure of protection, but not enough to relieve Crèvecoeur of fears for his own life and those of his two sons. In October he sent the boys to Le Havre to await passage to some place of safety. Ally was offered a job with an American merchant in Hamburg, but Louis was not able to escape until May, when he took passage for America, bought two hundred and twenty acres of land near the mountains west of Orange County, and undertook the life of an American farmer.

For Crèvecoeur, now living in Fanny's modest apartment in Paris, survival was a matter of shifts and expedients. He cultivated his American acquaintances, Gilbert Imlay in Le Havre and Joel Barlow in Paris among them, apparently seeking some avenue of escape to the United States. When James Monroe came to Paris in the summer of 1794 as the new American ambassador to France, Crèvecoeur's hopes rose. Fanny was an old friend of Mrs. Monroe, and he might make himself useful to her influential husband. He helped Monroe procure a country house for the summer, oversaw the making of an American flag for the embassy, and ran any other errand that was asked of him. At last he made his request: could Monroe give him some minor diplomatic mission that might serve as a pretext for his departure from France? Monroe, very cold and distant, cut him off short. With all hope of an American refuge shattered, Crèvecoeur returned to his father's house in Caen. In early November the final blow fell; in the aftermath of the fall of Danton, Otto was arrested and imprisoned.

Something of Crèvecoeur's state of mind during these desperate months can be seen in the bizarre code in which he corresponded with Ally. Dates are jumbled, letters are addressed from Pine Hill, the Elbe is renamed the Potomac, Crèvecoeur is called Cahio-Harra (the name the Indians had given him thirty years earlier), and his father becomes "the old Sachem."[23] The letters testify not only to Crèvecoeur's dangerous penchant for mystification—the code makes even this innocent correspondence suspect—but also to the continuing appeal of America to his imagination. Fifteen years before, he had made the Farmer of the *Letters* seek refuge from the storm of another revolution in the wilderness village of an Indian tribe. In France and caught in this more terrible storm, he dreamed again of an Indian metamorphosis, one that would transmute these survivors of the petty nobility of France into red men, free and heroic.

By early 1795, it was clear that the worst was over. Otto was released after six weeks of imprisonment and reinstated in his position. In May, Crèvecoeur was able to join Ally in Hamburg, where he spent a year of boredom and depression that was relieved only by visits with French *émigrés* who were passing through the port and by frequent dinners with Mary Wollstonecraft, who shared his dismal view of Hamburg society. In early 1796, he returned to France and retired to Normandy. The next four years were his most serene since the early days at Pine Hill. It was safe now for Louis to come home from the United States, and he was invited by Fanny and Otto to live with them at Lesches, their country house near Meaux. Crèvecoeur sent agricultural advice to them from Normandy, where he was at work on another book, a long examination of America and its significance in the guise of a fictitious travel-narrative. He wrote steadily, circulating portions of the manuscript among his family and friends for their criticism. The death of his aged father late in the next year permitted him to leave Normandy and join his family at Lesches. By then the new book was finished.

When an attempt to find an English publisher for it failed, he sent the work to a Paris firm, which issued it in three handsome volumes in early 1801 as *Voyage dans la Haute Pensylvanie et dans l'état de New-York*. Although it was far more carefully assembled and ambitiously designed than the *Lettres*, the *Voyage* attracted little attention. Crèvecoeur's lengthy examination of the civilization of America failed to interest a France disillusioned in the goals of the Enlightenment, a France which sought salvation in the dictatorship of Napoleon and which now viewed the New World chiefly as the locale of the romantic primitivism of Chateaubriand's *Atala*, published in the same year.

Otto, meanwhile, was enjoying a brilliant success. In October the great Treaty of Amiens, which seemed to insure permanent peace between England and France, and of which he was the chief negotiator, was signed in London. After a brief visit with Otto and Fanny there, Crèvecoeur returned to Lesches, where, living quietly on the farm, he corresponded with his friends and a wrote a few incidental articles on America. Despondent at the news of Ally's death in 1806, he joined Otto and Fanny in Munich. There, for the next three years, he studied German mechanical inventions, advised the Bavarians on the making of potato bread and the culture of fruit trees, and entered into the intellectual and artistic life of the capital. The activity of his mind is suggested by the range of his writings in Bavaria, which include a little Oriental tale in English for his granddaughter and an article on lightning rods for a Munich newspaper. But even in Bavaria violence intruded. In the spring of 1809 he was forced to flee to France before the advancing Austrian army.

Crèvecoeur's last years were spent in a charming country house which Otto had bought at Sarcelles. There he could visit the ancient Madame d'Houdetot at nearby Sannois and resent her latest satellite. Crèvecoeur could practice his beloved country occupations, interest himself in the most recent developments in textile machinery and steamboats, correspond with his favorite granddaughter, and read histories and narratives of travels. The only anxiety came in early 1813 when Louis, an officer with Napoleon's army on the retreat from Moscow, was not heard from for three months and was believed lost. But all else was tranquil. There was time for visits to Paris and Lesches, time to write a memoir of Madame d'Houdetot, who had died in January, for Ally's widow. In the fall Crèvecoeur suffered a recurrence of a heart ailment that had troubled him since his imprisonment in New York, more than thirty years before. On November 12, he died at Sarcelles. It was not a Christian death; the last rites were not administered, for the old man no longer held to the faith of his youth.

The life that had ended, with its motifs of evasion and disguise and its seeming dedication to the principle of self-preservation, could tempt one to accuse Crèvecoeur of cowardice—to see in his chameleon-like capacity to adapt himself to his surroundings a flabbiness of value and belief. But, before passing self-righteous judgments like these, one should acknowledge the extremity of the circumstances in which he again and again found himself, recognize the fact that two-thirds of his adult lifetime were lived amid the confusion of war and revolution, remember that imprisonment and violent death, dispossession and exile, were recurrent dangers in his own experience and in that of the people he loved.

And perhaps, too, one might consider the series of remarkable accidents that put him so often at the center of the storm and wonder if indeed they were mere accidents. One might contrast the vicissitudes of his career with his father's drably safe existence and ponder what it was that required him to abandon the secure routines of Normandy, to embark for America, to subject himself to the hardships of the wilderness and the labors of the farm, to seek out the risks of public life, to travel and to learn to the limit of his lifetime. Yet even his admiring great-grandson felt compelled to punctuate his characterization of Crèvecoeur with phrases like "prudent, timide," and to attribute to him an "esprit hypocondriaque."[24] Surely, he was fearful and impulsive under pressure; surely, he was no hero of melodrama.

The fact remains, however, that he time and again subjected himself to pressure, time and again exhausted his resources of nerve and strength. If, as his biographers agree, he was not "un très grand homme," not one of those personalities "qui s'imposent à l'admiration de la postérité,"[25] he used himself as if he were a great man. And, from that life of stress, from the ranging experience of his many roles, Crèvecoeur drew the complex insights and the broad awareness which inform the best of his writings and give them a measure of the greatness that he could not himself enact.

CHAPTER 2

Letters from an American Farmer:
Fact and Doctrine

THROUGHOUT its career, *Letters from an American Farmer*, Crèvecoeur's first published work and the primary basis of his claim to a place in American literature, has been valued chiefly as a document rather than as a work of art. With a side glance at the charm of its style, readers from the eighteenth century onward have turned to the book as a repository of information on the life and landscape of British North America on the eve of the Revolution and as a body of informal speculations concerning the nature and meaning of the American experience.

Only recently, and still suprisingly infrequently, have commentators on the book called attention to its equal interest as an essentially imaginative exploration of human experience, one that is not limited by the boundaries of America. In the late eighteenth and early nineteenth centuries, the book served Europe as one of its most influential vehicles of information about America and as a report on the application of the liberal and humane doctrines of the Enlightenment to a functioning society. In the late nineteenth and early twentieth centuries, the perspective broadened; for Crèvecoeur was gathering a reputation as a close observer of nature in the New World, as a remarkably early American exemplar of the feeling for nature; he had now become "the eighteenth-century Thoreau," all the more interesting because the setting of his nature notes was the remote milieu of the colonial era.

If, in the last thirty years, Crèvecoeur has become less the eighteenth-century Thoreau than the the eighteenth-century de Tocqueville, the change has come about because of a new interest in his contributions to the formulation of a theory of America and not because of a radical change of approach to his book. It is perhaps symptomatic that the great majority of modern readers who have any firsthand acquaintance with Crèvecoeur's writings know only the essay "What Is an American," the most commonly anthologized of all the chapters of the *Letters* and surely one of those most preoccupied with social reportage and commentary. The present task, then, is to examine the Farmer's role as observer and analyst of the American scene, to assess the documentary importance of the *Letters* as a record of colonial American experience and as an interpretation of its significance.

I *Some Local Information*

In introducing Crèvecoeur's first book to its English audience, the publishers stressed its interest as a source of facts about America. The letters, they announced, "are made public, because they contain much authentic information, little known on this side the Atlantic. They cannot, therefore, fail of being highly interesting, to the people of England, at a time when every body's attention is directed toward the affairs of America" ([v]). *Letters from an American Farmer* was to be received as the most recent contribution to a growing body of works which sought (or pretended) to supply the British reading public with reliable accounts of the land and peoples of the troublesome North American colonies.

For the most part these works, like Andrew Burnaby's *Travels through the Middle Settlements in North America* (1775) and Jonathan Carver's immensely popular *Travels through the Interior Parts of North America* (1778), belonged to the ancient genre of narratives of travel and exploration, but a few focused their attention on important single facets of America; two such works, James Adair's *History of the American Indians* and the anonymous *American Husbandry*, had been published in London in 1775. But, as yet, no account of the American environment had been rendered by a participant in the process of settlement, one who had not merely witnessed but had experienced the daily life of the American colonist. The American Farmer of Crèvecoeur's book presented himself as just such a source of "local and unadorned information." Whatever the Farmer might lack in general knowledge and in philosophic sophistication, "I can describe," he modestly declared, "our American modes of farming, our manners, and peculiar customs, with some degree of propriety, because I have ever attentively studied them" (2).

What is needed, the Farmer tells Mr. F. B., the correspondent to whom his letters are addressed, is a systematic survey of American society in all its manifestations. But he himself lacks the knowledge, the intellectual discipline, and the literary skill that are required by such a task. His method must be more impressionistic and selective than that of the thoroughgoing social analyst. He cautions Mr. F. B. not to look for "the style of the learned, the reflections of the patriot, the discussions of the politician, the curious observations of the naturalist, the pleasing garb of the man of taste"; instead, Mr. F. B. is to find the "spontaneous impressions" of a "cultivator of the earth," a man who can follow only "the line which Nature has herself traced for me" (20).

A survey of the contents of the *Letters* suggest that Nature's line is indeed a devious one. The opening letter serves as an introduction in that it establishes the circumstances of the Farmer's correspondence with Mr. F. B. and suggests the point of view of the succeeding letters. Letter II consists of an informal and impressionistic report "On the Situation, Feelings, and Pleasures, of an American Farmer" as the narrator has experienced them on his farm in central Pennsylvania. The third letter, "What Is an American," attempts to answer the query of its title by taking a sweeping survey of the impact of America on the European immigrant, a survey which sketches the diversity of American life but which concentrates on the rural culture of the middle colonies.

Letters IV–VIII describe in detail the manners and customs of the whaling villages of Nantucket and Martha's Vineyard, while the ninth letter gives a brief account of Charleston, South Carolina, and the consequences of slavery. Letters X and XI return the reader to the middle colonies, first for some sketches of the birds and snakes on the narrator's farm and then for the report of a Russian gentleman on his visit to John Bartram, the celebrated Pennsylvania naturalist. The book concludes with a letter in which the Farmer pictures in highly emotional colors the disruption of his life by the outbreak of the Revolution and expresses his intention of fleeing with his family to an Indian village in the remote wilderness.

The bulk of Crèvecoeur's "authentic information" on British North America is thus organized around his descriptions of three widely separated and sharply differing areas of settlement: the villages and farms of the middle colonies, the maritime communities of Nantucket and Martha's Vineyard, and the plantation society of South Carolina. His methods for portraying these three geographic and economic sectors vary considerably. The rural life of the middle colonies is developed chiefly by accounts of individual experience, the Farmer's own, and that of other representative colonists. The whaling villages of the Massachusetts islands are approached by more conventional means: the discursive exposition of the local historian and the detailed reports of the touring observer. Limited to a single letter, the treatment of the slave society of Charleston takes still another form; it is a combination of generalized, summary description and a single, sharply drawn scene.

II The South and Slavery

As reportage, Crèvecoeur's treatment of the last of these three sectors of American life is the least consequential. Its paucity of factual detail probably indicates that whatever information on South Carolina he possessed came to him second-hand. He had traveled southward to Virginia in 1776, an excursion which presumably furnished the materials for the "Sketches of Maryland and so on Southerly" that he had lost during his imprisonment in New York;[1] but there is no evidence that his tour had taken him as far south as Charleston. Indeed, there is nothing in Letter IX that could not have come from Crèvecoeur's readings, from his conversations with friends like Tétard, formerly minister of the French Reformed Church in Charleston, and from his own lively imagination.

As Howard Rice has pointed out, the opening generalized portrait of Charleston as the Lima of the North owes much to the account of the Peruvian capital in the Abbé Raynal's *Histoire philosophique des deux Indes* (1770).[2] Like Raynal, to whom Crèvecoeur dedicated the *Letters* and on whom he apparently relied heavily as a source of information and ideas while writing it, the Farmer focuses on the debilitating effects of a warm climate and of wealth too easily procured. The Farmer's view of the city is distant and disapproving: its "inhabitants are the gayest in America; it is called the center of our beau monde, and is always filled with the richest planters in the province," men who surround themselves with luxuries little known in other parts of North America, for "the rays of their sun seem to urge them irresistibly to dissipation and pleasure" (214, 215). If the Carolinians are not priest-ridden like their counterparts in Latin America, they have subjugated themselves to an equally parasitic element in their society, the lawyers, whose wealth and influence in South Carolina foreshadow the day when "the law will possess in the north what now the church possesses in Peru and Mexico" (216). Thus the main burden of Crèvecoeur's remarks on Charleston is the contrast between the plantation society of the South and the norm of American life. The simplicity, moderation, and wholesome equality that characterize the tenor of society in the other British colonies and constitute the unique promise of America are missing; in Charleston, the New World is already old.

But the sketch of Charleston does afford Crèvecoeur the opportunity to comment on Negro slavery, an institution which was distinctively American and which was becoming a subject of increasing interest and concern to the European audience that the *Letters* addresses. While slavery had become almost an obligatory topic for any writer on America by the third quarter of the eighteenth century, the passion and force of Crèvecoeur's remarks suggest that his response to the subject was more than routine. In spite of the fact that he, like most prosperous farmers in the middle colonies, kept slaves at Pine Hill, it would seem that he was familiar with the growing body of anti-slavery literature and had embraced its cause. In Raynal's *Histoire,* a virtual compendium of the humanitarian ideas of Voltaire, Rousseau, Diderot, and the other *philosophes* of the French Enlightenment, Crèvecoeur had encountered "an eloquent and powerful advocate" of the cause "of the poor Africans," as his dedication to Raynal points out ([x]). Moreover, as an admirer of the simplicity and humanitarianism of the Quakers, he was well acquainted with "the remonstrances of several Friends, and of the good books they have published" on the subject of slavery (262)—writings from the pens of men like John Woolman and Anthony Bénézet, who had made slavery a vital moral issue in the colonies during the decades immediately preceding the Revolution and who had prompted the Society of Friends to recommend the manumission of slaves to its membership in 1754 and to require it in 1772.[3]

Although Crèvecoeur holds up "the good Quakers" as models of right action toward Negroes, the bases of his argument against slavery are philosophical rather than religious. As in all of his speculations, the Farmer's thoughts on slavery center on the concept of nature, nature as it is evinced in the order and tendency of the external universe and as it manifests itself in the primal feelings, needs, and rights of mankind. And again, as in most of the Farmer's speculations, that concept of nature takes on radically inconsistent forms as the discussion progresses. At first, the macrocosm of external nature and the microcosm of human nature are set forth as standards by which the evil of slavery may be measured. Slavery is to be condemned because it is profoundly unnatural. The system by which the "chosen race eat, drink, and live happy, while the unfortunate one grubs up the ground, raises indigo, or husks the rice: exposed to a sun full as scorching as their native one, without the support of good food, without the cordials of any cheering liquor" (216–17), violates the natural principle of justice. "Strange order of things!" the Farmer exclaims. "O Nature, where art thou?—Are not these blacks thy children as well as we?" (217). By its disruption of family life, by its denial "of those ineffable sensations with which nature inspires the hearts" of parents and their children, slavery forces Negroes into an "unnatural state"; "the very instinct of the brute, so laudable, so irresistible, runs counter here to their master's interest; and, to that god, all the laws of nature must give way" (218–19).

But, as the Farmer turns to the contrast between slavery in the North, where Negroes are often given a rudimentary education and exposed to the influences of religion, and the brutal exploitation of slaves by the plantation system of the South, he abandons his appeal to instinct and natural law. Now the natural state is associated with primitive savagery, with violence and uncontrolled rapacity. Southern slavery is to be condemned, not because it runs counter to nature, but because it fails to rise above nature. Its victims "are left in their original and untutored state; that very state, wherein the natural propensities of revenge and warm passions are so soon kindled" (223). Still more dismaying are the effects of slavery on the masters, for—whether in the North or the South, whether ancient or modern—slavery encourages those who profit by it to indulge their most brutal impulses. Indeed, as the Farmer totals the hardships with which nature afflicts mankind and the cruelities which men inflict upon each other, he finds it more and more difficult to cling to his trust in the beneficence of God's creation.

The furthest limit of this headlong plunge into pessimism is reached with the nightmarish little vignette that concludes Letter IX. Ostensibly offered as an example of the atrocities perpetrated by the plantation system of South Carolina, the scene is in reality an emblematic image of the human condition as the Farmer's foregoing dark meditations have described it. On his way to dinner at an outlying plantation, the Farmer comes upon an appalling sight. A Negro is imprisoned in a crude cage suspended from a tree, his body lacerated by birds of prey and stung by swarms of insects. The Farmer gives him water, regretful that he lacks the means to put an end to the Negro's misery.

Upon reaching his destination, the Farmer learns that the slave is being punished for having killed the overseer of the plantation: "They told me that the laws of self-preservation rendered such executions necessary; and supported the doctrine of slavery with the arguments generally made use of to justify the practice; with the repetition of which I shall not trouble you at present" (235). These quiet words, with their undertone of absolute contempt for the formulas by which the plantation owners try to justify themselves, conclude the letter by returning it to the specific issue of slavery.

But, on the way to that ending, Crèvecoeur has led his readers into speculations that far transcend the immediate implications of slavery, and he has gone well beyond his promise to convey the "local and unadorned" facts of life in America. There can be no doubt that the scene of the caged Negro is one of the most powerful and memorable in the book, as the frequency with which it was reprinted in Crèvecoeur's day and the critical attention that it has attracted in our own testify. But the very artistry and surrealistic force of the scene argue against its basis in literal fact. The abruptness with which it is introduced, its strange transmutation of the animal imagery that appears in previous letters, the richness of its thematic implications, all suggest that it is a major instance of the shaping and creating power of Crèvecoeur's imagination, not the product of his experience.

This suggestion is strengthened by the contrast between the pace and tone of the account of the caged Negro and those of a parallel passage that appears in one of the English manuscripts which Crèvecoeur omitted from the *Letters*. The Farmer is complaining of the mosquitoes that infest the coastal areas of America:

> Mr. .... informed me that a farmer of ...., in order to punish his negro, had thought proper to tie him naked to a stake in one of his salt meadows. He went home, where he staid but twenty-three minutes. At his return he found his negro prodigiously swelled, in consequence of the repeated stings of millions of mosquitoes which he had received. He brought him back to his house, but all his care could not prevent an inflammatory fever of which he died. (*Sketches*, 110)

In this passage the dispassionate voice and eye for detail of the reporter are fully in evidence. The object is merely to convey information, information not acquired by firsthand observation, it is true, but nevertheless to be assembled and recounted with scrupulously literal accuracy. This mode is noticeably absent from Letter IX,[4] an absence which suggests not only that Crèvecoeur had little or no direct experience with the life of the deep South but, more importantly, that he had no interest in constructing a detailed, documentary report of Southern society. Lacking firsthand information, he could have turned to the observations of others for the necessary data. But the South, in Crèvecoeur's eyes, was exotic and atypical, notable chiefly for the contrast it offered to the habits and values which seemed to him to be characteristically American. Insofar as Letter IX contributes to the depiction of American experience, its function is to establish a foil to the sturdy and humane life of the farmers and fishermen of the North, a life which the *Letters* records at close range and in full detail.

III *The Whalemen*

Those who know the *Letters from an American Farmer* only by reputation and excerpt are likely to be surprised by the fact that approximately one third of the text is allotted to an account of Nantucket and Martha's Vineyard. That the Farmer, the celebrator of the soil and the plow, the spokesman for the inland counties of the middle colonies, should choose to record in full detail and at great length the life of a people devoted to the sea may at first seem an anomaly. The description of the whaling communities serves, it is true, to further the announced intention of suggesting the diversity of American social and economic patterns; surely the maritime and commercial communities of New England are appropriate to the scheme.

Yet if the treatment of plantation society is too skimpy and impressionistic to offer a balanced representation of the Southern face of America, the five solid letters that deal with Nantucket and Martha's Vineyard are disproportionately specific and inclusive. Moreover, the patterns of life on the sandy coastal islands of Massachusetts were (and are) more picturesque than typical, more extraordinary than representative. For the purpose of illustrating the mercantile societies of the maritime North, a survey of Boston, Salem, Newport, or New London would have been more to the point. Once again, it would seem, the scheme of representing the three principal areas of colonial life merely permits Crèvecoeur's peculiar approach and emphasis; it does not account for them.

Perhaps the simplest explanation of the decision to supply a lengthy, detailed account of Nantucket and Martha's Vineyard is that the islands offered Crèvecoeur the opportunity to examine in detail two topics of immediate interest to the European reader: Quakerism and the Yankee whale fishery. The Quaker communities of the New World had long been admired by Old World intellectuals and humanitarians as models of a society ordered on principles of simplicity and benevolence. From Voltaire forward, the French *philosophes* had used the gentle Quakers as important weapons in the assault upon religious formalism and intolerance, political violence and injustice, and social artificiality and complexity.

Raynal's *Histoire philosophique* in itself could have indicated to Crèvecoeur the significant role that the sect played in the European imagination. Since Nantucket had been originally settled by Quakers and still offered, by reason of its isolation, remarkably pure examples of Quaker customs and manners, the island gave Crèvecoeur the opportunity to examine at close range a functioning Quaker society. Throughout the letters on Nantucket the Farmer pays strict attention to the benign effects of the beliefs and practices of the sect. The harmonious relations between the Quakers and their Congregationalist neighbors, the devotion to sobriety and industry, the democratic simplicity, and the meek obedience to the law which he finds all corroborate the European concept of the Quakers.

If Quakerism, like slavery, was an obligatory topic for the commentator on America, the whale fishery was rapidly becoming another one. The astonishing success of American whalemen, operating with little capital and without governmental subsidy, was a matter of acute interest in the latter half of the eighteenth century to European powers, which saw in the fishery not only a source of profit but an important nursery for the seamen needed to man their expanding navies. In the Parliament of England and in the ministries of the French government, the efficiency and enterprise of the Yankee whalers were held up as models for emulation.

Aware of the importance of whaling as the first area of economic activity in which Americans had demonstrated a clear superiority over their European competitors, Crèvecoeur gives considerable space to the exposition of American whaling techniques: the methods of finance, the system of training seamen, the types of equipment, the kinds of whales that are pursued, and the tactics by which they are captured. And from all the data, the most detailed information which the book offers, emerges an almost Melvillean celebration of the heroic audacity of the hunters, of the wonder "that so slender a vessel as an *American whale-boat,* containing six diminutive beings, should dare to pursue and attack, in its native element, the largest and strongest fish that nature has created" (154).

Important though the subjects of Quakerism and whaling are to the letters on Nantucket and Martha's Vineyard, they are subordinate to a still larger concern. They lend a note of topical interest to this section of the book, but here, as throughout the *Letters,* reportage is finally subsumed under Crèvecoeur's grand design: the construction of a theory of America. And it is only in relation to the attempt to define the broad significance of the settlement of the New World that the sustained focus on the two whaling communities becomes fully justified. Early in the opening letter on Nantucket, the Farmer states the thesis which underlies the entire section: the island, "barren in its soil, insignificant in its extent, inconvenient in its situation, deprived of materials for building . . . seems to have been inhabited merely to prove what mankind can do when happily governed" (116). The true promise of America, the implication is, consists not in immense natural resources, not in the prospect of quick and easy wealth, but in the opportunity to construct a society that will permit man to fulfill his best possibilities.

The sandy islands of Massachusetts offer, then, ideal conditions for demonstrating the principle that the happiness of America is the product of its institutions rather than its natural gifts. Nature is hostile and niggardly on Nantucket, "a barren sand-bank, fertilized with whale-oil only" (173). The sole benefits of the natural environment are negative; the islanders need never arm themselves against conquest, for their lands offer no temptation to the greedy. Nor need they fear internal corruption, for it "is but seldom that vice grows on a barren sand like this, which produces nothing without extreme labour. . . . This land must necessarily either produce health, temperance, and a great equality of conditions, or the most abject misery" (148-49).

In this negative way, the natural environment is an important condition of the humane and moderate communities of the islands. The contrast between them and the lush degeneracy of Charleston is pointed, for, to a degree, Crèvecoeur is faithful to the doctrinaire environmentalism which Montesquieu had propounded in *The Spirit of the Laws* and which Raynal had echoed in his *Histoire.* Indeed, Crèvecoeur's book, as a whole, is grounded on the principle that it announced in Letter III: "Men are like plants. The goodness and flavour of the fruit proceeds from the peculiar soil and exposition in which they grow. We are nothing but what we derive from the air we breathe, the climate we inhabit, the government we obey, the system of religion we profess, and the nature of our employment" (53-54). But, as the wording of this passage indicates, the physical environment of soil, topography, and weather, the sole determinants of the life of the plant, comprises only a portion of the system of influences which shape the life of man. Political, religious, and economic institutions are also a part of the metaphoric soil and exposure that govern human growth. And although, as Montesquieu had argued, those institutions may be modified by geography and climate, they are not wholly determined by physical circumstances. Thus a poor land like that of Nantucket may forbid the growth of luxury and dissipation, but it does not guarantee the establishment of sturdy and just societies. The crucial determinant of happiness or misery is ultimately human, it would seem, not natural.[5]

That Nantucket is no sandy Eden, no special sanctuary of virtue and happiness, is made clear by the Farmer's account of the Indians who had previously occupied the island, and who for centuries had warred bitterly against one another, very nearly to the point of extermination. The present peace and prosperity of the island spring not from the soil but from the particular form of society that the whalemen have evolved, a society which, unlike its Indian predecessor, has made the achievement of a harmonious order its major goal. The islands offer the closest approach to what Crèvecoeur would seem to regard as an ideal society, and therefore they demand a sustained and searching scrutiny.

The result of that scrutiny is Crèvecoeur's only full-blown attempt to picture a whole society, to trace its origins and development, to survey its "customs, religion, manners, policy, and mode of living" (118). He analyzes the economic system of the islands at length, studying the balanced interrelationship of farming, the wool industry, the whale fishery, and external commerce; outlining the complex system of land ownership; and delineating the roles of the various occupations within the total economic structure. He investigates courting and marriage customs, and he records the islanders' amusements and recreations. Habits of dress and speech, the odd and nearly universal addiction to whittling, the more dangerous but less common fondness for opium—all these details help to characterize the society. But more important than the picturesque peculiarities of Nantucket and

Martha's Vineyard are the basic principles on which their society is grounded, principles which make the islands a model for the right ordering of any human community.

A prime source of stability and continuity in the islanders' sensible mode of life is the high respect that they hold for the family. Not only is the population at large bound together by a network of familial relationships, but within the individual household the family unit is strong and binding. Unlike most sailors, the men of the islands are married. Not driven to sea by desperation or by an irresponsible thirst for adventure, they regard the ocean as "a kind of patrimony; they go to whaling with as much pleasure and tranquil indifference, with as strong an expectation of succes, as a landsman undertakes to clear a piece of swamp" (171).

The children, as well as the men, are led into the paths of duty and order by the family, for the family is the chief instrument of education on the islands. In Crèvecoeur's modest Utopia, academic learning can function only as a disturbing element: "it would pervert their plain judgement, it would lead them out of that useful path which is so well adapted to their situation: it would make them more adventurous, more presumptuous, much less cautious, and therefore less successful" (174). Like the beehive, to which the Farmer compares the island communities, the ideal human society functions without confusion or coercion, and without change. The highest intellectual attainment for which the islanders should strive is "good sense, improved upon the experience of their fathers; and this is the surest and best guide to lead us through the path of life, because it approaches nearest to the infallibility of instinct" (174). Experience and example take the place of authoritarian indoctrination; "by the force of example, which is superior even to the strongest instinct of nature, more than by precepts" (151), the island children are taught to adopt the attitudes and values of their parents, and the environment itself prepares them for their future occupation: "Those children, born by the sea-side, hear the roaring of its waves as soon as they are able to listen; it is the first noise with which they become acquainted, and by early plunging in it they acquire that boldness, that presence of mind, and dexterity, which make them ever after such expert seamen" (176-77). Schooled in perfect acquiescence to the mores of their parents and instilled with an affection for the dangerous livelihood on which the community depends, the children enter maturity perfectly equipped to perpetuate the established mode of life.

In a society comprised of individuals so trained, external sanctions and restraints may be relaxed. Although the varying fortunes of a maritime economy make for sharp differences in wealth, the inhabitants of Nantucket and Martha's Vineyard are not saddled with a rigid class structure and a system of economic subservience. The accidental inequalities of wealth have introduced "neither arrogance nor pride on the one part, nor meanness and servility on the other" (172). The simple forms of the Quakers and the Congregationalists require no elaborate and costly system of ecclesiastical government.

Most extraordinary of all is the mildness of the civil government of the islands. The mother country wisely leaves the islanders to conduct their own affairs; the customs collector is the only royal agent to visit their shores. The burden of government within the society is equally light, for the Farmer could find "neither ostentatious magistrates, nor any individuals clothed with useless dignity: no artificial phantoms subsist here, either civil or religious; no gibbets loaded with guilty citizens offer themselves to your view; no soldiers are appointed to bayonet their compatriots into servile compliance" (147). The simplicity of the laws and the justice with which they are administered relieve the community from the plague of lawyers which infests other parts of America. Here "a man may pass . . . through the various scenes of a long life, may struggle against a variety of adverse fortune, peaceably enjoy the good when it comes, and never, in that long interval, apply to the law either for redress or assistance" (190-91). Here government and citizenry exist in perfect harmony: "Happy the people who are subject to so mild a government! happy the government which has to rule over such harmless and such industrious subjects!" (193).

Thus Nantucket and Martha's Vineyard define the true promise of America. The New World offers space, space that may be no more than a tiny spit of sand in the ocean, but room enough for the foundation of a new and better society. "After all," the Farmer asks, "is it not better to be possessed of a single whaleboat, or a few sheep-pastures; to live free and independent under the mildest government, in a healthy climate, in a land of charity and benevolence; than to be wretched, as so many are in Europe, possessing nothing but their industry; tossed from one rough wave to another; engaged either in the most servile labours for the smallest pittance, or fettered with the links of the most irksome dependence, even without the hopes of rising?" (175). The last significance of the islands is universal: teach men to restrain their ambitions and discipline their desires; give them a government that permits and encourages them to pursue their legitimate interests; and "What has happened here has and will happen every where else" (120).

IV *The American Farmer*

For the Farmer, who gives his address as "Carlisle, in Pennsylvania," the middle colonies are home ground, as they were for Crèvecoeur himself. Throughout the *Letters* the rural life of Pennsylvania, New Jersey, and New York provides the standard frame of reference for Crèvecoeur's description of America and his analysis of its meaning. While the treatment of the life of the middle colonies, scattered as it is among the various subjects of the first three letters and the last four, lacks the system and unity of the account of Nantucket and Martha's Vineyard, it nevertheless is held together by several loose strands of coherence. For one thing, the focus is on the experience of the individual.

If Nantucket and Martha's Vineyard had given Crèvecoeur the opportunity to study the community as a functioning organism, here he concentrates his attention on the careers, feelings, and attitudes of three rather concretely individualized Americans: the Farmer himself in Letters I, II, X, and XII; the typical immigrant Andrew, the Hebridean, in Letter III; and the naturalist John Bartram in Letter XI. Moreover, the major figure of this portion of the *Letters* is the one which Crèvecoeur's persona represents, the American as farmer. Not whaling and the sea but agriculture and the soil were at the center of life as it was experienced in the middle colonies and throughout most of America. For Crèvecoeur, however, the farmer was important not only as the representative American but as a pattern for all mankind. Indeed, the passages of the *Letters* that deal with the middle colonies become a virtual hymn to husbandry.

Crèvecoeur was writing at a time when interest in agriculture, both in England and on the Continent, was at its peak. For two centuries governments had looked to commerce and manufacturing as the mainstays of the national economy, but increasingly throughout the eighteenth century various schools of agrarian theorists, of whom the Physiocrats in France were the most notable, were proposing a shift of emphasis to agriculture as the true source of national wealth and as the foundation of the stability and happiness of the populace. Concurrently, the application of scientific knowledge to agriculture was transforming farming from a folk art into a technology. Writers like Arthur Young, the influential English expositor of agricultural improvement, were producing a substantial body of manuals and treatises on the new techniques and were stimulating a new interest among wealthy landowners in agricultural experimentation. The country was no longer a place to be shunned by the fashionable but a laboratory in which the public spirited and scientifically inclined gentleman might test techniques that would advance the prosperity of himself, his tenants, and his nation.

The "agricultural fad" in the latter eighteenth century, as one writer has termed the movement,[6] was both encouraged by and reflected in the new literary treatment of rural life that is one important element of the tendency toward Romanticism in the century. In English literature conventional pastoral poetry and Horatian praises of rural retirement steadily gave way to a more realistic mode of depicting country scenes and occupations. Increasingly the literature of the eighteenth century came to focus on the actualities of rural life; and, at the same time, it more and more discovered in the farmer the "natural man," man uncorrupted by the perversions and artificialities of civilization, man ennobled by close and essential contact with the wisdom and beauty of nature. Thus in *Die Wirthschaft* (1761), published in English as *The Rural Socrates* (1770), Hans Caspar Hirzel held up the Swiss peasant Kliyogg for his reader's admiration; for in Kliyogg could be found "the most exalted faculties of the human soul, in that state of noble engaging simplicity, void of pretension and ostentation, such as nature's plastic hand had formed us."[7] And in his *Histoire philosophique,* the Abbé Raynal had made the connection between this exaltation of farming and the promise of the New World crystal clear:

It is in the colonies that men lead such a country-life as was the original destination of mankind, best suited to the health and increase of the species: probably, they enjoy all the happiness consistent with the frailty of human nature. We do not, indeed, find there those graces, those talents, those refined enjoyments, the means and expense of which wear out and fatigue the springs of the soul, and bring on the vapours of melancholy which so naturally follow an indulgence in ardent pleasure: but there are the pleasures of domestic life; the mutual attachments of parent and children; and conjugal love, that passion so pure and so delicious to the soul that can taste it and despise all other gratifications. This is the enchanting prospect exhibited throughout North America.[8]

Raynal's thought is precisely that which underlies Crèvecoeur's treatment of the life of the middle colonies in the *Letters*.

Letter I immediately establishes the identity and authority of Crèvecoeur's persona, the American farmer James, by presenting him as the agrarian natural man. Uncertain whether he should respond to the request of his English friend, Mr. F. B., for a series of reports on life in America, the Farmer fears that his lack of knowledge and sophistication disqualifies him for the task. He gains confidence from his minister's assurance that plowing and wisdom are wedded, that, "as we silently till the ground, and muse along the odoriferous furrows of our low lands . . . the salubrious effluvia of the earth animate our spirits, and serve to inspire us" (14-15). The Farmer's authority as observer and as interpreter derives from this inspiration, which more than compensates for his lack of formal learning and the limited range of his experience.

More than that, the minister asserts, Mr. F. B.'s request affords the Farmer the most interesting and pleasing subject imaginable; for his task is to depict the activities and accomplishments of "a race of cultivators," men who, like himself, are engaged in the construction of an agrarian society. The minister tells the Farmer that he must not regret the fact that the colonies offer little of the romantic appeal in which the ancient ruins and rich traditions of Europe abound:

Here . . . every thing is modern, peaceful, and benign. Here we have had no war to desolate our fields. Our religion does not oppress the cultivators. We are strangers to those feudal institutions which have enslaved so many. Here nature opens her broad lap to receive the perpetual accession of new comers, and to supply them with food. I am sure I cannot be called a partial American when I say, that the spectacle, afforded by these pleasing scenes, must be more entertaining, and more philosophical, than that which arises from beholding the musty ruins of Rome. . . . Here we have, in some measure, regained the ancient dignity of our species; our laws are simple and just; we are a race of cultivators; our cultivation is unrestrained, and therefore every thing is prosperous and flourishing. For my part, I had rather admire the ample barn of one of our opulent farmers, who himself felled the first tree in his plantation, and was the first founder of his settlement, than study the dimensions of the temple of Ceres. I had rather record the progressive steps of this industrious farmer, throughout all the stages of his labours and other operations, than examine how modern Italian convents can be supported without doing any thing but singing and praying. (7–9)

The minister thus at once justifies America as a literary and philosophical subject on the grounds of its modernity and prosaic practicality, the very basis of the complaint that American writers in the nineteenth century were to register against their native land; and it also outlines the approach which the Farmer is to take toward that subject, one which is to be firmly embedded in the general exaltation of rural life. Farming is the proper occupation of mankind; America, by its newness, its abundance, and its benign social institutions, offers mankind a unique opportunity to pursue that sacred task.

Letter II, "On the Situation, Feelings, and Pleasures, of an American Farmer," supplies an intimate, impressionistic account of the color and texture of the narrator's daily life as a freeholding farmer in Pennsylvania. Although the method of the letter differs sharply from the objective, reportorial manner that Crèvecoeur employs in his account of Nantucket and Martha's Vineyard, the chief values of the life that is here displayed are much the same as those which the letters on the islands had stressed. Thus the isolation and simplicity of the Farmer's existence strengthen the ties of family and, in so doing, afford him a succession of small delights. He can recall the early days of his marriage when his wife "would often come with her knitting in her hand, and sit under the shady tree, praising the straightness of my furrows and the docility of my horses. This swelled my heart and made every thing light and pleasant . . ." (23).

Now, as he contemplates his wife by the hearth "while she either spins, knits, darns, or suckles our child, I cannot describe the various emotions of love, of gratitude, of conscious pride, which thrill in my heart, and often overflow in involuntary tears" (25). He is fond of taking his little boy with him into the fields, where he places the child on a seat attached to the plow:

> As I lean over the handle, various are the thoughts which croud into my mind. I am now doing for him, I say, what my father formerly did for me: may God enable him to live that he may perform the same operations for the same purposes when I am worn out and old! I relieve his mother of some trouble while I have him with me; the odoriferous furrow exhilarates his spirits, and seems to do the child a great deal of good, for he looks more blooming since I have adopted that practice. Can more pleasure, more dignity, be added to that primary occupation? The father, thus ploughing with his child, and to feed his family, is inferior only to the emperor of China ploughing as an example to his kingdom. (27)

Like the children of Nantucket, who from birth hear the sound of the sea, the Farmer's son is schooled in the natural environment from which he is to win his livelihood and his happiness. His education comes not from books but from the soil; he learns not by precept but by experience.

Like the men of Nantucket, the Farmer leads a life that is securely rooted in the natural world. The seasonal cycle and the successive phases of animal life are a perpetual source of awe and pleasure to him. The summer combats of the kingbirds and the bees, the frolic of the snow buntings in the depth of winter, and the swarming flight of insects in the spring fascinate the Farmer and astonish him as manifestations of the miraculous processes of nature. The farm, like the whale fishery, produces "true Christians," men too impressed by the majesty of the natural creation and its Creator to quarrel over differences in religious dogma and practice.

This idyll of domestic felicity and of natural harmony is a consequence not of sensibility alone but also of prosaic economic circumstances. The Farmer's sense of security and stability, his confident assumption that his son will inherit the farm and perpetuate the values that he has been taught, his eager acceptance of the difficult labor that the improvement of his property demands, his ability to identify himself with his land and the natural life that it supports—all stem directly from the fact that he owns the soil he tills. Unlike the Russian serf or the English tenant, the American farmer is a freeholder, and that makes all the difference:

> The instant I enter on my own land, the bright idea of property, of exclusive right, of independence, exalt my mind. . . . What should we American farmers be without the distinct possession of that soil? It feeds, it clothes, us: from it we draw even a great exuberancy, our best meat, our richest drink; the very honey of our bees comes from this privileged spot. No wonder we should thus cherish its possession: no wonder that so many Europeans, who have never been able to say that such portion of land was theirs, cross the Atlantic to realize that happiness! This formerly rude soil has been converted by my father into a pleasant farm, and, in return, it has established all our rights. On it is founded our rank, our freedom, our power, as citizens; our importance, as inhabitants of such a district. These images, I must confess, I always behold with pleasure, and extend them as far as my imagination can reach; for this is what may be called the true and the only philosophy of an American farmer. (25–26)

The philosophy which the Farmer here endorses is what historians have labeled the "freehold concept." As Chester E. Eisinger has pointed out, the concept embraces three major principles: that "every man has a natural right to the land"; that "through ownership of the land the individual achieves status and self-fulfillment"; and that "the good political society must provide for the uninhibited development of the farmer."[9] A natural outgrowth of the eighteenth-century idealization of the farm and the farmer, the concept was to occupy a central position in the ideology of Jeffersonian democracy and be enshrined in the institutions and national attitudes of the republic that was soon to take shape, as the present official encouragement of agriculture in the face of enormous farm surpluses may serve to remind us. In *Letters from an American Farmer,* the concept is already fully formulated and firmly identified with the unique promise of life in America.

The content of that promise receives its most extensive and explicit statement in Letter III, "What Is an American." Placing the middle colonies at the center of his panorama, the Farmer attempts first to isolate the essential general characteristics of American life and then to show their impact on the experience of the individual by means of the history of Andrew, a fictitious but representative new American. The premise of the letter is a bold one: "We are the most perfect society now existing in the world" (48). Most of the leading features of the general society are those that characterize the microcosmic communities of Nantucket and Martha's Vineyard: a mild and beneficent government, a modest and widely shared prosperity, a striking absence of crime, and a tolerance of religious diversity.

But in an agrarian economy, as opposed to a maritime one, the system of land tenure assumes a crucial importance. Like the device of lays, by which the crew of a whaling vessel shares in the profits of the voyage, American freehold farming stimulates individual effort and initiative "because each person works for himself" (47). Moreover, the lands that American farmers possess "confer on them the title of freemen, and to that title every benefit is affixed which men can possibly require" (50). Small wonder, then, that the European immigrant, leaving behind him a country "that had no bread for him; whose fields procured him no harvest; who met with nothing but the frowns of the rich, the severity of the laws, with jails and punishments; who owned not a single foot of the extensive surface of this planet" (49), looks toward America as the promised land.

The central concern of Letter III thus becomes the "surprising metamorphosis" by which the European is transformed into the American, "this new man" (51). That metamorphosis is an absolutely radical one, "a sort of resurrection" (73): "[The American] is neither an European, nor the descendant of a European. . . . He is an American, who, leaving behind him all his ancient prejudices and manners, receives new ones from the new mode of life he has embraced, the new government he obeys, and the new rank he holds. He becomes an American by being received in the broad lap of our great *alma mater*. Here individuals of all nations are melted into a new race of men, whose labours and posterity will one day cause great changes in the world" (51-52).

The new man and the new race arise from the new environment, both geographical and social. "I know," the Farmer insists, "men are nothing of themselves, and that they owe all their different modifications either to government or other local circumstances" (83). In this most buoyant section of the *Letters*, environmental determinism becomes a source of immense reassurance. The New World and the new society that has been constructed in it, the most nearly perfect in existence, have the capacity to redeem the European from his misery, to work a change in him as total as the transition from death to life. But even here, Crèvecoeur's commitment to environmentalism and the cheerful assurance that it generates are qualified and diminished by counterstatements. Not all immigrants experience a saving rebirth. Indeed, some "have mouldered away their time in inactivity, misinformed husbandry, and ineffectual endeavours" (77). How is one to account for the fact that some newcomers succeed and others fail? Perhaps national origin has something to do with it, for German and Scotch immigrants generally fare better than those from Ireland. Perhaps, too, individual intelligence, energy, and strength of character play a more decisive role than the doctrine of environmentalism admits. The accents in which the New World welcomes the immigrant sound a note of warning as well as of promise: "Go thou, and work, and till; thou shalt prosper, provided thou be just, grateful, and industrious" (87).

If America offers no guarantee of automatic success, it nevertheless seems to insure the reward of virtue. The career of Andrew, the Hebridean, supplies an extended demonstration of how a poor European can advance "from indigence to ease; from oppression to freedom; from obscurity and contumely to some degree of consequence—not by virtue of any freaks of fortune, but by the gradual operation of sobriety, honesty, and emigration" (88). Landed on the dock at Philadelphia, Andrew is befriended by the Farmer, who arranges for the immigrant and his family to live and work as hired laborers on a farm near the Pennsylvania frontier. There, in the course of a year, Andrew learns the skills of American farming and saves enough money to lease land for his own farm. With his neighbors' help, he clears his fields and builds his house, laboring with such success that by the end of four years his property is worth $640. He is an established citizen, a freeman, and a minor officer of the local government. Thus the Farmer has traced the gradual transformation of the European, trained to poverty and humiliation, into the American, the confident possessor of the happiness and dignity that rightfully belong to all men.

If Andrew represents the average product of the American experience, Letter XI offers a portrait of an exceptional man: the American in his fullest development. The letter, the only one which employs a persona other than the Farmer, is the report by a touring Russian gentleman of a visit of several days with John Bartram at the famous botanist's farm on the banks of the Schuylkill. As the sketch of Bartram proceeds, it becomes apparent that he, in his character and in his way of life, embodies the best features of the American life that the earlier letters had depicted. Letter XI thus serves to review and bring together the values which for Crèvecoeur constitute the essential significance of the new society and the new man that America has brought into being.

First and foremost, Bartram is a farmer. When the Russian visitor first encounters him, the venerable naturalist, dressed in the wide trousers and leather apron of a common laborer, is hard at work with a gang of men constructing a levee. His farm is a model one, a working demonstration of what the diligence and progressive agricultural methods of a freeholding farmer can achieve. As a farmer, Bartram remains a natural man, despite his impressive scientific knowledge and his international renown. His interest in botany began when he was plowing a field one day and paused to examine a daisy. The complexity of the structure of the flower aroused his curiosity, and he determined to educate himself in the science that would allow him to satisfy it. Over the years he became the foremost authority on the flora of America, corresponded with the learned societies of Europe, and was honored by the attention of Queen Ulrica of Sweden. But Bartram has retained his modest simplicty; he can only marvel that the Queen "should think in her palace at Stockholm, of poor John Bertran on the banks of the Schuylkill" (258-59.)[10]

Bartram is a Quaker as well as a farmer, another exemplar of the humane and simple sect that Crèvecoeur, with his disregard for theology, regularly associates with the natural religion of the Deists. The prayers that are said at Bartram's dinner table are "divested of the tedious cant of some, and of the ostentatious style of others" (250). The Russian attends a meeting of the Friends with his host and admires the tidy plainness of the meetinghouse, the quiet sincerity of the congregation, and the good looks of a woman who is moved to speak, "very handsome, although upward of forty" (261). Good Quaker that he is, Bartram has emancipated his slaves, pays them fair wages, and seats them at his table. With just treatment and the dignity of free men, they have "become a new set of beings" (263). Thus Bartram's household becomes a microcosm of American society at large, a happy union of freedom and order; and Bartram himself emerges as the ideal representation of that new man, the American.

This account of the visit to Bartram, with its images of serene order and unpretentious prosperity, completes the main development of Crèvecoeur's depiction of the middle colonies and, as it does so, brings to a conclusion the whole panoramic view of the new civilization that has grown up in British North America. The life which that view encompasses is not quite an unadulterated idyll, for the horrendous vision of the Negro in the cage in Letter IX is a reminder that man in the New World can be as vicious and cruel as he ever was in the Old World.

Moreover, the American environment poses certain unique threats to the moral stability of its inhabitants. In Letter III, in the course of a discussion of the successive steps by which a new country is settled, the Farmer glances briefly at the life of the frontier. Those who inhabit the outermost fringes of white settlement undergo a disturbing degeneration. Surrounded by the predatory animals of the wilderness, they become predators themselves, abandoning agriculture, the basis of a stable and humane society. Crèvecoeur's frontiersmen foreshadow the sinister figures of Cooper's Ishmael Bush, Bird's Nick of the Woods, and Melville's Colonel Moredock; they are killers who spawn "a mongrel breed, half civilized, half savage" (64). Lawless, irreligious, and indolent, they have reverted to the primitive state from which an orderly society alone offers redemption.

But the shadows that darken the otherwise sunny prospect of America are transitory. Slavery must give way before the enlightened humanitarianism which the Quakers have heralded. And the brutal life of the backwoodsmen is only a temporary phase of the process of settlement, for "Time will efface those stains: in proportion as the great body of population approaches them, they will reform, and become polished and subordinate" (68). In the long view, then, the image of America that the first eleven letters construct is bright indeed, "one diffusive scene of happiness, reaching from the sea-shores to the last settlements on the borders of the wilderness" (193).

But in the twelfth letter, the last of the book, that happy scene is blotted out. Letter XII, "Distresses of a Frontier-Man," returns to the intimate, intensely personal mode of Letter II; but the placid inventory of pleasures and satisfactions that constitute the life of an American farmer is here replaced by a nearly hysterical recital of fears and woes. The outbreak of the Revolution has destroyed the fabric of the Farmer's existence and shattered the society on which he depends. His farm is exposed to the ravages of British raiding parties, and he and his family are terrorized by nightmare visions of the torch and the scalping knife. His neighbors demand that he choose sides in the conflict, but he feels loyalty for the mother country and for the community now in rebellion against her. In desperation he has determined to abandon his farm, the product of "the accumulated industry of nineteen years" (291), to sever himself from the society that has been the object of his study and admiration, and to seek the refuge of an Indian village in the remote wilderness. There he will plant his crops and rear his children, doing his best to preserve them from the seductions of the Indian way of life. Letter XII thus works a total reversal of what would seem to be the movement of all that has preceded it. The idea of America as an asylum from poverty and oppression, as the site of a new ordering of society and the birthplace of a new race of men, is swept away in a torrent of despair and denial.

The cry of anguish with which *Letters from an American Farmer* ends cannot be approached and comprehended by reference to the system of explicit facts and ideas by which Crèvecoeur constructs his description of America and his interpretation of its significance. Letter XII belongs to a still larger scheme, one that is not limited to the materials on America. Here the question is no longer, "What is an American?" but "What is Man?" That second question, however, is not posed for the first time in Letter XII. All along, just beneath the surface of exposition and analysis, it has seethed and churned, making its presence felt in the image that takes on symbolic weight, in the anecdote that borders on parable, in the intricate play of motifs that extends throughout the heterogeneous materials of the letters. But only in Letter XII is the reader forced to confront this larger significance of the book. Crèvecoeur's exploration of the enigma of man is conducted with such indirection in the preceding letters that its presence may go undetected in a casual reading of the book. On its most accesible level, the book remains a pleasantly discursive commentary on the nature and meaning of the American experience.

V *The Value of the Document*

Insofar as it is simply a book about America, *Letters from an American Farmer* constitutes a sufficiently remarkable achievement. Viewed in the context of other eighteenth-century attempts to describe and explain the society of British North America, Crèvecoeur's book is most impressive in its over-all design and effect, in its extraordinarily successful integration of fact and doctrine. Taken singly, however, neither the body of information nor of ideas in the *Letters* represents a particularly useful or profound contribution to the comprehension of the New World. The reader who turns to the book as a source of information is apt to be more struck by what Crèvecoeur omits than by what he includes.

He offers no description of urban America; Boston, New York, and Philadelphia—standard topics in the reports of European travelers in America—receive scarcely a mention in passing. He has nothing to say of the territories west of the Appalachians, although his service in the French army had equipped him to exploit that wide interest in the wilderness and the Indians to which books like Carver's *Travels* appealed. With the exception of the letters on Nantucket and Martha's Vineyard, Crèvecoeur's sketches virtually ignore matters of geography, history, politics, and economics, the basic material of surveys like Raynal's *Histoire philosophique*. His treatment of such topics as slavery and the Quakers elicits little information with which the well-read European would not already be familiar. Even American agriculture, the one subject on which Crèvecoeur's persona is an authority, gives rise to very few hard facts. We know that the Farmer studies the play of instinct in the behavior of his cattle, but we never learn what their breed is. We know that he seats his little boy between the shafts of his plow, but we are not told what crops he plants.

Nor is the structure of ideas on which Crèvecoeur erects his analysis of America noteworthy for its originality or its strength. Everywhere in the *Letters* the reader recognizes echoes of Voltaire, of Montesquieu, of Rousseau. An index of the doctrines which the Farmer espouses on one occasion or another would form a compendium of the intellectual clichés of the latter eighteenth century and seem certain evidence that the *Encyclopédie* was a tool as essential to him as his mattock. But surely Howard Rice is right in his suggestion that Crèvecoeur, at least in the period of his residence in America, had little direct acquaintance with the great literature of the Enlightenment and that his stock of ideas came to him from the pages of Raynal's *Histoire*.[11]

The resemblance of the *Letters* to the *Histoire* in both general philosophical assumptions and attitudes and in specific intellectual positions can scarcely be overstated. The celebration of agriculture as the basis of human happiness and prosperity and of the British North American colonies as the hope of mankind and the asylum for the oppressed of Europe are fundamental to both books. Both works waveringly and tentatively assert the superiority of the natural over the artificial, using the wisdom of instinctual behavior and the attractiveness of primitive life for white captives of the Indians as evidence. Both identify the family as the basic source of legitimate pleasure and social stability. Both regularly attack the clergy and the legal profession as parasitic sowers of discord and champion the Quakers as models of simplicity and humanitarianism. Both fervently condemn Negro slavery as well as all other forms of injustice and exploitation. Both find British rule in North America to be mild and salutary and look with disfavor toward rebellion against it. At almost every point, Raynal offers a striking parallel to the ideas which find expression in the *Letters.* The words of Crèvecoeur's dedication to Raynal are no empty compliment:

> A few years since, I met, accidentally, with your *Political and Philosophical History,* and perused it with infinite pleasure. . . . You viewed these provinces of North America in their true light: as the asylum of freedom, as the cradle of future nations, and the refuge of distressed Europeans. Why, then, should I refrain from loving and respecting a man whose writings I so much admire? These two sentiments are inseparable, at least in my breast. I conceived your genius to be present at the head of my study: under its invisible, but powerful, guidance, I prosecuted my small labours; and now, permit me to sanctify them under the auspices of your name. ([ix]– [xi])

It would be fatuous to contend that Crèvecoeur's basic response to America and his judgment of its significance were derived from Raynal; most probably they antedated the influence of the *Histoire,* just as they most certainly outlasted all evidences of specific debts to Raynal. But beyond any doubt Crèvecoeur found in Raynal not only authoritative confirmation of his own opinions but in many instances the particular formulations and applications which he gave them in the *Letters.* Truly, Raynal was his tutelary genius.

If Crèvecoeur was heavily indebted to Raynal's popularization of the doctrines of the *philosophes* for the intellectual framework of the *Letters,* his use of those doctrines is anything but systematic. Certain examples of inconsistency in idea have been pointed out in the course of this chapter, chiefly in connection with the handling of environmentalism and the appeal to nature as an ultimate standard. Indeed, so baffling are the reversals of position in the *Letters* that, while one commentator can find good evidence for labeling Crèvecoeur a true follower of Rousseau in his glorification of Indian life,[12] another can contend that "he was never guilty of the fanciful idealization of Indian life that was characteristic of some of the French followers of Rousseau."[13] Still another cautiously observes that Crèvecoeur was "such a man of moods that no single passage, on whatever theme, can safely be taken as an index of his convictions on the subject."[14] Up to a point, the conflicting statements of the *Letters* seem to be reflections once again of the influence of Raynal. The position of the *Histoire philosophique* is a moderate one that tempers its protests against the abuse of government with passages on the virtues of obedience and balances its comments on the delights of the state of nature with tributes to the blessings of civilization. But what Raynal suggests as a possibility, or poses as a question, the Farmer sometimes assumes as a certainty, thereby converting Raynal's alternative hypotheses into contradictory doctrines. While this clash of idea and attitude tightens the tension and heightens the dramatic force of the *Letters* as a work of art, it weakens the coherence of the book as a work of exposition and analysis.

As such a work of exposition and analysis, what, then, is the value of the *Letters*? Perhaps a definition of that value can best be approached by returning to Crèvecoeur's statement of his relation to Raynal in the Dedication of the *Letters*. There he modestly contrasts his own comprehension of America as "an humble American planter, a simple cultivator of the earth" ([ix]), with the sweeping researches of the learned Abbé. The not-so-modest implication, fully justified by the actual accomplishment of the *Letters*, is that his comprehension is the fruit of experience, of actual contact with the soil and society of America, and hence has an authenticity and authority that no distillation of documents can possess. Crèvecoeur's book is the first full-scale attempt by an American to describe and explain his country. Reared in another culture and writing at the moment when a sense of the common character and destiny of the British colonies of North America was first emerging, Crèvecoeur was able to attain the awareness of the colonies as an organic whole that hitherto had found expression only in the writings of foreign observers and analysts.

But, unlike those foreign commentators, he had lived and worked, married and reared a family, on the ground that he was to survey. Thus his book is able to make the generalizations and theoretical abstractions of the *Histoire philosophique* come to life. It reports what it is like to live three thousand miles removed from the central government, how the sense of freedom enters into the smallest thoughts and most trivial plans of a man in that lucky situation; for the Abbé, badgered and threatened by the royal authorities for his liberal opinions, such freedom could only exist as an idea. At his best, Crèvecoeur again and again transforms Raynal's doctrines into experiences, translating the tenets of agrarianism into the way one looks at the child by the hearth or into the pleasure one takes in the taste of honey.

But, insofar as Raynal contributed to the formulation of those doctrines that the Farmer's life enacts, his service to Crèvecoeur was great indeed. If those ideas, regarded in isolation seem merely the commonplaces of the Enlightenment, they take on a compelling significance in the context of the *Letters*. For into the fabric of the daily experience and fundamental attitudes of the actors of the *Letters*—the Farmer, the immigrant Andrew, the islanders of Nantucket, John Bartram—Crèvecoeur has woven the strands of those humane and hopeful ideas which, in the setting he gives them, we can recognize as the components of the American Dream. The America and the American that the *Letters* delineates foreshadow with striking completeness and precision the characteristics and values that in the nineteenth and twentieth centuries were to be enshrined as national ideals.

Saturated in the ideology of the Enlightenment, Crèvecoeur carries the explication of the significance of America far beyond the expectation of economic opportunity that the promotional tracts of the colonial era had held out or the promise of political justice and freedom that the pamphlets of the Revolutionary decade were enunciating. Crèvecoeur's America is not only the seat of prosperity and freedom; it is the home of a virtuous simplicity, an innocence that is nourished by close contact with the soil and with nature and by insulation from the outworn institutions and the disrupting innovations of Europe.[15] It is the field of religious diversity and toleration, a place where men honor good will and good deeds more than the subtleties of theological distinctions. It is the asylum for the poor and oppressed of other nations, a sanctuary that is inexhaustible in its space and opportunity. Above all, it is the melting pot from which a new man is forged—a man exempt from the burden of history; a man free of guilt, misery, and deprivation.

Letters from an American Farmer represents, then, a remarkably early and a remarkably complete formulation of the major items of the national faith. Still more striking is the fact that it articulates those bright hopes not in abstract statement alone but in a series of delightful and plausible images that spring from what is offered as the common experience of common men. But, most impressive of all, its complex art steadily and insidiously reveals the distance between the new man of theory and the old man of reality.

CHAPTER 3

Letters from an American Farmer:
Form and Theme

U NTIL recently, any discussion of Crèvecoeur as a conscious literary artist has been forestalled by the traditional judgment that *Letters from an American Farmer* is a work of charming artlessness. The primary quality which commentators have found in the book is sincerity, a sincerity conceived of as the direct expression of thoughts and feelings, undistorted by the formal arrangement and obliquity of art. The apparent lack of structure, the seemingly crude and abrupt shifts in mode, the childlike preoccupation with birds and insects, and the unabashed emotionalism of the *Letters* have been offered as examples of that artlessness and celebrated as evidence of that sincerity. Surely no man so unconcerned with the demands of order, no man so lacking in artifice and control could be anything less than a truth-teller. The whole value of the *Letters* seemed predicated on lack of form and complexity.

This view of the *Letters* was encouraged by Crèvecoeur himself. Not only does the book employ the persona of the natural man, the simple cultivator of the earth whose lack of sophistication is testimony to his honesty; but Crèvecoeur habitually blurred the distinction between that persona and its creator. Received upon his return to France as "un sauvage américain," he did nothing to correct the impression that he was in the most literal sense the American Farmer of his book; for that role was the basis of his appeal to the fashionable circle which took an interest in him and offered him the support he desperately needed. For a century and a half the world accepted Crèvecoeur's posture of naïve sincerity at its face value. The standard judgment of the *Letters* was formed in the decade of its publication when Meister, in the great *Correspondance littéraire*, declared the book to be "written without system and without art, but full of interest and sensibility"; its value lay in its "simple and truthful pictures," the "expression of an honest soul."[1] That judgment, perpetuated in the paragraphs of literary histories and the headnotes of anthologies, remains the dominant one to this day.

A small but important band of commentators has challenged the prevailing view. In an introduction to an edition of the *Letters* published in 1904, Ludwig Lewisohn suggested that the book "differs from other works descriptive of early conditions in America in that it should be regarded primarily as a piece of literature," and in *Expression in America* (1932) he found the *Letters* to manifest "a skill approaching subtlety."[2] In an article first published in 1919, D. H. Lawrence discovered Crèvecoeur at his best to be an authentic artist, one whose art "is in terms of the great sensual understanding, dark and rich."[3] If other critics have not shared Lewisohn's view of the *Letters* as an exquisite pastoral idyll or felt in it the pulse of Lawrence's blood-knowledge, they nevertheless have become increasingly aware of its artistry.

In an angry response to the detection of signs of deliberate shaping and manipulation of materials in the *Letters*, John Brooks Moore in 1925 contended, with perfect justice, that "the self-consciousness which such artifice reveals in the artist should prevent us from any longer looking upon Crèvecoeur as a delightfully ingenuous child of nature."[4] Two years later, recovered from his initial shock, Moore could praise Crèvecoeur as "a genuine (though not a first-rate) artist,—certainly, if not our only artist of the eighteenth century, our only tolerably consistent one"; now, looking back on the *Letters*, he wondered if perhaps "the whole book has more fiction in it than meets the first perusal."[5]

More recent critics, embracing without hesitancy or regret the hypothesis that the *Letters* may be a work of art, have begun to give the book the close critical scrutiny which that hypothesis requires. Marius Bewley has employed the scene of the caged Negro as a model of symbolic technique, demonstrating Crèvecoeur's effective use of subjective distortion, ironic contrast, and veiled allusion.[6] In what is beyond question the best single article on Crèvecoeur that has yet appeared, Albert E. Stone approaches the *Letters* as a fable expressive of the conflict of dream and reality, a prototype of the American romance. Insisting that the book is not to be read as history or autobiography but as embryonic symbolic fiction, Professor Stone opens the way to a radically new analysis of Crèvecoeur's technique and to an important reappraisal of the place of the *Letters* in the history of American literature.[7]

I *The* Letters *and Their Writer*

Among the most obvious rewards of an approach to the *Letters* as a work of the imagination is the perception of a degree of structural unity not otherwise apparent. Beyond the general plan of displaying the three principle areas of British North America, the book is singularly lacking in logical organization, the minimum expectation that one brings to expository writing. Even the loose tripartite plan is disjointed in its execution, for the letters that deal with the middle colonies are interrupted by the series on Nantucket and Martha's Vineyard and by the single letter on Charleston. But if one shifts one's attention from the Farmer's information to the Farmer himself—viewing him as a specific (if fictitious) individual who is engaged in writing letters in response to the requests of a foreign friend, and who, at the same time, is subjected to the vicissitudes of his own experience—a meaningful order emerges.

The basis of that order resides in the epistolary form which encompasses the book. Whether or not the series of sketches which compose the *Letters* originated, as Crèvecoeur later contended, in an actual correspondence, the retention of the epistolary form in the book as it was finally published in itself constitutes a departure from straightforward exposition and the adoption of an ordering principle that is essentially imaginative. The device of the letters, it is true, is fairly common in eighteenth-century books of travel; but rarely does it perform any organic function; the apparatus of correspondence could be deleted without effecting the substance or the tone of the work.

Crèvecoeur's employment of the epistolary form, however, more closely resembles its use in the novels and imaginary voyages of the century than in the narratives of actual travels. In novels like Richardson's *Pamela* (1740) and Rousseau's *Julie* (1761), or in imaginary voyages like Montesquieu's *Persian Letters* (1721), the personality and point of view of the letter writer become at least equal in importance to the events and objects on which he reports. The letter writer functions not only as a reporter, a medium through which images of the external world are transmitted, but also as a literary character endowed with a particularized and significant sensibility, equipped with a background of past experience, and meaningfully involved in the world that his letters reveal.

Crèvecoeur's adoption of the epistolary form, then, has several important consequences. At the very minimum, it helps to justify the lack of logical order in the *Letters*. The book is constructed on the pretense that the Farmer is engaged in a two-way exchange of letters with his English acquaintance, but we are permitted to see only half of the correspondence, his own contributions to it. For the most part, however, Mr. F. B. is in control of the correspondence; he is the one who initiated it, and his rather random requests set the topics for the majority of the letters.

Two of the letters, significantly the darkest of the entire series, are prompted by the impact of the Farmer's own immediate experience rather than by the inquiries of Mr. F. B. Letter IX, on Charleston and slavery, takes its substance and tone from the Farmer's shocked response to his discovery, "not long since," of the caged Negro, a sight by which "my mind is, and always has been, oppressed since I became a witness to it" (232). Still more urgent is the nearly hysterical tone of the last letter, in which the Farmer conveys his newly formed decision to retreat into the wilderness from the society that is collapsing around him. The course of the *Letters* is thus determined by two impulses, neither of which bears any relation to the organizational requirements of systematic exposition: the demands of the Farmer's correspondent and his own reactions to his present experiences.

The epistolary form, however, is far more than a strategem by which Crèvecoeur excuses his violations of logical organization; by serving as the vehicle of characterization and narration, it spins its own strands of coherence. Scattered through the letters are bits of self-revelation which, pieced together, establish the Farmer as a concretely realized individual, a figure endowed with a depth and complexity sufficient to persuade us that he moves and breathes and is not merely the mask through which the auctorial voice speaks. His name is James, and he owns outright a farm close to the eastern slopes of the Allegheny Mountains in Pennsylvania, presumably at Carlisle, on "the edge of the great wilderness, three hundred miles from the sea" (10).

His grandfather, a Presbyterian, had emigrated from England, bringing with him a "few musty books"—"Scotch divinity, the Navigation of Sir Francis Drake, the History of Queen Elizabeth, and a few miscellaneous volumes" (2). James's father, "a plain-dealing, honest man . . . one of yea and nay, of few words" (17), had bequeathed his son "three hundred and seventy-one acres of land, forty-seven of which are good timothy meadow, an excellent orchard, a good house, and a substantial barn" (23). Receiving that inheritance as a young man, James had been repelled by the tedium and heavy labor of farming; for a time, he had taken up the solitary life of an Indian trader in the employ of his uncle, and had planned to sell the farm. But freedom has its terrors:

> [W]hen I came to consider myself as divested of my farm, I then found the world so wide, and every place so full, that I began to fear lest there would be no room for me. . . . Why should not I find myself happy, said I, where my father was before? . . . I married; and this perfectly reconciled me to my situation. My wife rendered my house all at once cheerful and pleasing: it no longer appeared gloomy and solitary as before. When I went to work in my fields, I worked with more alacrity and sprightliness. I felt that I did not work for myself alone, and this encouraged me much. (22–23)

By the time that he begins his correspondence with Mr. F. B., James has been settled on his farm for over ten years. His wife has developed a sharp tongue and a strong will, and she is far from happy about the task which Mr. F. B. has imposed upon her husband. Surely the neighbors will suspect him of trying to curry political favor through this correspondence with a great Englishman or, still worse, of harboring literary ambitions: "How would'st thee bear to be called, at our country meetings, the man of the pen? If this scheme of thine was once known, travellers, as they go along, would point out to our house, saying, Here liveth the scribbling farmer" (18-19). Yet she has been a good wife to James: "no woman was ever a better oeconomist, or spun or wove better linen" (292). She is, he observes in his last letter, "the best gift" that God has given him (317).

James's blessings are many. His farm is a productive one: "Every year I kill from 1500 to 2000 weight of pork, 1200 of beef, half a dozen of good wethers in harvest; of fowls my wife has always a great stock: what can I wish for more?" (23-24). His wife has a kitchen wench to help her, and James has several slaves to aid in the work of the farm. The couple has a daughter and at least three sons. James has bought a farm as a dowry for his daughter who, by the time of the last letter, is soon to marry. For his oldest son, he has purchased a large tract of land in the wilderness, hoping that the country will be settled when the boy is ready to marry. Another son is destined for the ministry, and the youngest will inherit the family farm.

That James has the leisure and means to indulge his taste for travel is evidenced by his trips to Massachusetts and South Carolina. He takes particular delight in studying the process of settlement, making frequent journeys to any new settlement that he hears of. Indeed, he has "caused upwards of a hundred and twenty families to remove hither. Many of them I have led by the hand in the days of their first trial . . ." (292). But this modest affluence and patriarchal authority have not been won without skill, labor, and foresight. By the time he writes his last letter, James has invested nineteen years of steady labor in his farm, clearing the forests and draining the swamps for the plow and the scythe.

The life that James has achieved by his industry and wisdom is the embodiment of that serene good order and natural simplicity which Crèvecoeur identified with the best possiblities of the American experience. Profoundly non-political, James owns allegiance to both the large community which comprises the British Empire and the small community of his native land; he seeks to disengage himself from the quarrels between them, wishing only to be "an useful subject; ever obedient to the laws, ever vigilant to see them respected and observed" (292). He is still more profoundly nonsectarian. He diligently instructs his family and his neighbors in their duty to God and man by expounding the Decalogue; but religious sects are, in themselves, a divisive force: "Each worship with us hath, you know, its peculiar political tendency" (312-13). Unconcerned with religious and political factionalism, James devotes himself to the fulfillment of his obligations as husband, father, neighbor, and subject.

This indifference to ideological controversy is less the result of policy than of temperament. The center of James's life, the core of his being, is the play of sensation and emotion, not the clash of ideas and the thrust of action. "Sentiment and feeling," he confesses, "are the only guides I know" (277). James, like some sensitive instrument, responds to and registers each nuance of change in the atmosphere around him. But, unlike the instrument, he takes delight in the process of response and seeks to prolong and vary it. The life that he has constructed on his farm is in every way designed to maximize the exquisite pleasure that he derives from exploring the range of tender feelings inspired by his family and from savoring the beauty and mystery of nature. He is, as Mr. F. B. has pointed out, "the farmer of feelings" (24) more than of corn and timothy—the careful husbandman of evocative images and the cultivator of sentiment.

Just as he clears his fields and drains his marshes, making wildness tractable, so he builds his life on the principles of order and stability, shielding himself as effectively as he can from the intrusion of any experience that by its intensity or violence might shatter the delicate instrumentation of his sensibility. He is a watcher of small creatures, of hummingbirds and ephemerae; he is not an assaulter of whales, like the men of Nantucket. The "ever-raging ocean" is too much for him, a power that crowds in upon his senses and paralyzes him: "[The sea] irresistibly attracted my whole attention; my eyes were involuntarily directed to the horizontal line of that watery surface, which is ever in motion, and ever threatening destruction to these shores. My ears were stunned with the roar of its waves, rolling one over the other, as if impelled by a superior force to overwhelm the spot on which I stood. My nostrils involuntarily inhaled the saline vapours which arose from the dispersed particles of the foaming billows, or from the weeds scattered on the shores" (208).

Irresistibly, involuntarily, the Farmer, stunned and nearly overwhelmed, is fixed in passive contemplation, caught in a stasis much like the one that overtakes him in his confrontation with the Negro in the cage; there "I found myself suddenly arrested by the power of affright and terror; my nerves were convulsed; I trembled, I stood motionless, involuntarily contemplating the fate of this negro in all its dismal latitude" (234). This "characteristic paralysis of will," as Professor Stone terms it,[8] is evidence of James's terrible vulnerability, of the danger that experience holds for him. For, though the will is paralyzed, the mind seethes with activity, generating a stream of "gloomy thoughts" (232) that sweeps him into confusion and sometimes into despair. James enjoins his correspondent in his final letter: "Do not imagine . . . that I am a stoic; by no means. . . . Would to God I was master of the . . . tranquillity of that magnanimous sect" (298-99). For James, serenity is more than a philosophical preference; it is the condition of psychic survival.

That Crèvecoeur's portrait of James is something other than literal autobiography is obvious. Few of the details of the history or situation of the American Farmer tally with what is known of the experience of the proprietor of Pine Hill. Only on the deeper level of temperament and sensibility does James offer insights into the nature of his creator, and even there one must discount the distortions of heightening and emphasis. Indeed, the relation between Crèvecoeur and James is comparable to that which exists between the novelist and the central intelligence which he may employ as his narrative medium; and it should be approached with the caution that critics of fiction have learned to exercise. It is apparent also that James functions in the *Letters* as something more than the conventional persona, or mask, so often employed in eighteenth-century persuasive prose. Transcending the role as the mouthpiece of its creator, the mask of the *Letters* assumes a life of its own. As has been seen, the Farmer is not merely a voice and a general point of view; he becomes, indeed, an object of interest in himself, a figure endowed with all the potential for experience and response that one expects to encounter in the characters of a work of fiction. That potential, moreover, is not permitted to lie dormant in the *Letters*. Taken as a whole, the series of letters implies a line of action, a succession of experience so relevant to the characterization of James that it may be termed a rudimentary plot. Regarded from this perspective, the organization of the book suggests that Crèvecoeur was by no means "a chronicler of unrelated episodes," as he has been called,[9] but a writer capable of constructing a sustained narrative of an action that has a beginning, a middle, and an end.

II *The Story of James*

Although there is no strict correspondence between the chronology of the *Letters* and the sequence of actual events,[10] the broad movement of James's experience parallels and in large measure is determined by the course of history. The book opens in the narrative present, as James reports the family debate that Mr. F. B.'s request for a series of letters on America had provoked. Only a few vague hints indicate that it is the eve of the Revolution: James's wife has seen the speeches of "friend Edmund" in the newspapers, presumably Burke's great speeches of 1774 and 1775 on the colonial problem; and she fears that her husband's correspondence with a prominent Englishman like Mr. F. B. will arouse the suspicion of the colonel of the local militia. But the setting of Letter I is otherwise unclouded.

The bucolic idyll of Letter II narrows James's world to the farm, where all, at least in the realm of human life, is serene and beneficent. Letter III extends the idyll to America as a whole, as James surveys the process by which the new man is brought to life and goes about the performance of his duties as midwife to that spiritual rebirth. In an anecdotal mood, he reports the observations on American settlement that he has made over the last eight years; and rarely in the view, except in the backward glances at Europe, is there a scene of suffering or an object of terror. There is, to be sure, a passing reference to Indian massacres along the frontier; but the Indians which James has encountered in the wilderness are genial fellows: "I shook hands with them, and I perceived they had killed a cub; I had a little peach brandy, they perceived it also, we therefore joined company, kindled a large fire, and ate a hearty supper" (96).

The vigorous life that the five letters on Nantucket and Martha's Vineyard describe is no less idyllic, but the account of it is even more clearly tied to the recollection of the past than are the materials of Letter III. Nowhere in the series is there any indication that James's visit to the islands has been recent. Instead, the perspective is that of memory, a memory separated from the visit by a length of time sufficient to permit James to invest his recollections with a logical coherence and system found nowhere else in the *Letters*. More important, the islands are only tangentially related to his own experience. He has been there, but as a tourist and not as an inhabitant and participant. By contrast to what has gone before them, the five letters thus convey a striking sense of detachment, of distance between the observing consciousness and the objects of its observation. In their faint suggestion of the alienation of James from his environment, they signal a crucial change in the movement of the *Letters*.

The violence of that change becomes apparent in Letter IX, on Charleston, where the idyll gives way to the hell-scene. The dominant images of the letter are the reverse of those that have gone before: here the sun burns too brightly, the climate is debilitating, and life is either sumptuous and corrupt or unbearably painful. The full horror of the place is epitomized in the macabre scene of torment that concludes the letter; but, before it appears, one is given James's response to it: the flood of anguished thought that plunges him into pessimism, utterly eclipsing his former bright vision of the golden future of man in America. His doubts are ultimate ones. Contemplating the spectacle of man's indifference to his own cruelty, he begins by posing the question of human nature: "What, then, is man? this being who boasts so much of the excellence and dignity of his nature, among that variety of inscrutable mysteries, of unsolvable problems, with which he is surrounded?" (220).

And enigma follows enigma: "Is there . . . no superintending power who conducts the moral operations of the world, as well as the physical? The same sublime hand, which guides the planets round the sun with so much exactness, which preserves the arrangement of the whole with such exalted wisdom and paternal care, and prevents the vast system from falling into confusion, doth it abandon mankind to all the errors, the follies, and the miseries, which their most frantic rage, and their most dangerous vices and passions can produce?" (225).

This contrast between the serene order of the natural universe and the chaotic violence of the human world now becomes the focus of James's speculations. Man converts the garden that nature provides him into a waste land:

The history of the earth! doth it present any thing but crimes of the most heinous nature, committed from one end of the world to the other? We observe avarice, rapine, and murder, equally prevailing in all parts. History perpetually tells us of millions of people abandoned to the caprice of the maddest princes, and of whole nations devoted to the blind fury of tyrants; countries destroyed; nations alternately buried in ruins by other nations; some parts of the world, beautifully cultivated, returned again into their pristine state; the fruits of ages of industry, the toil of thousands, in a short time destroyed by few! If one corner breathes in peace for a few years, it is, in turn, subjected, torn, and levelled. (225–26)

Man is here the sole agent of evil, the disrupter of order and the destroyer. In almost Calvinistic terms, James finds the springs of human action "to be poisoned in their most essential parts"; for "Man, an animal of prey, seems to have rapine and the love of bloodshed implanted in his heart" (226).

As the stream of thought rushes on, it undercuts still further the confident assumptions on which James has built his life. Nature itself now appears chaotic, destructive, malignant: "In the moments of our philanthropy we often talk of an indulgent Nature, a kind Parent. . . . Yet, if we attentively view this globe, will it not appear rather a place of punishment than of delight? . . . Famine, diseases, elementary convulsions, human feuds, dissensions, &c. are the produce of every climate; each climate produces, besides, vices and miseries peculiar to its latitude" (228). The global survey yields one nightmarish image after another; the polar "voids, where nothing lives; regions of eternal snow; where Winter in all his horrors has established his throne"; "the parched lands of the torrid zone, replete with sulphureous exhalations"; "the poisonous soil of the equator," with its "putrid slimy tracks [tracts], teeming with horrid monsters, the enemies of the human race" (229). "On this little shell," James exclaims, "how very few are the spots where man can live and flourish!" (230).

This hellish vision of chaos and violence marks the crisis of the book. Superficially, it is James's shocked response to the atrocities of slavery; but, more meaningfully, it signals the moment at which he first consciously challenges the validity of the idyll which the earlier letters had bodied forth, the moment of a monstrous disillusionment. Ranging far beyond the specific issue of slavery, the flow of tormented speculation leads to a world in which convulsion and catastrophe are the norms of experience, and in which order and happiness come only as brief intervals in the reign of turmoil and anguish. Thus the full horror of Charleston for James is that it eradicates the distinction which he has drawn between America and Europe and on which he has founded his faith in the New World as the locus of a new life. And, for the reader, the letter, abounding as it does in images of warfare, both literal and figurative, presages the onslaught of the Revolution and with it the shattering of the serenity of the farm and of the America of which the farm is the microcosm.

From this point forward in the *Letters,* James cannot return to the sunny prospects of the early sketches. Ostensibly, Letter X, "On Snakes; and on the Humming-Bird" attempts to make just such a return. Once again the landscape is the pleasant fields and woods of James's home-country, and he again takes us with him on his investigations of the animal life of the neighborhood. But it is an infested landscape, a locale where beauty is the mask of a sinister violence. In rocky places near water lurks the copperhead snake, whose bite can first transform a man into the image of itself and then kill him. There are rattlers, the fangs of one of which, embedded in a boot, caused the death of both a father and his son. There is the swift and lovely black snake, harmless to human beings but gifted with the power to fascinate birds and squirrels and lure them into its jaws. Even the tiny hummingbirds, gorgeous in their dazzling colors, sometimes rip apart the flowers with unaccountable rage and fight each other to the death "with the fury of lions" (243). The letter closes with a long, vivid account of a battle between a black snake and a water snake, an extended image of convulsing violence and instinctive hatred, so intense that it becomes "uncommon and beautiful" (244). The angle of James's vision has altered drastically since Letter II. The natural world which is now revealed to him is no longer one over which he benevolently presides, tempering the winds of cruelty and hardship, but one of deadly beauty, which he watches with a passive fascination strangely like that of the victims of the black snake.

Letter XI, the record of the visit to Bartram, occupies an anomalous position in the book. In tone and substance it recalls the first three letters. The scene is rural Pennsylvania, that "flourishing province" pervaded by "a diffusive happiness" (247). In the setting, as in Bartram's life and character, all is tranquil and benign. But here Bertram and *his* way of life take over from James the task of exemplifying the dreamlike perfection of America. Indeed, James enters the letter only as the person to whom it is addressed. For once the narrating voice, the awareness, and the responses are those of another; and significantly they are those of a European, the touring Russian gentleman Mr. Iw———n Al———z.

This shift in persona serves several immediate purposes: it permits the interviewer to be acquainted with Bartram's European reputation; it allows him to draw a brief and undeveloped analogy between Russia and America as new countries having glorious futures before them; and it gives the whole letter the perspective of a well-traveled sophisticate who, by his ecstatic response to the American scene, seems to confirm the earlier impressions conveyed by the provincial James. But these minor services seem insufficient recompense for the disruptive effects of the shift. It constitutes an abandonment of the basic pretense on which the book depends for its authority, the stance of the native inhabitant; and it thus violates the logic of the correspondence, for Mr. F. B., who has himself performed an extensive tour of the American colonies and "knows most of our famous lawyers and cunning folks" (4), would surely find a measure of redundancy in a European visitor's interview with an American celebrity. The Farmer's function is to supply his own impressions, not to retail those of another tourist.

But, to the reader who is concerned with the submerged plot of the *Letters* and is attentive to the dynamic relationship between belief and experience in the consciousness of James, the intrusive voice of the Russian gentleman sounds overtones that are of immense relevance to the general movement of the book. Letter XI becomes an ominous interlude during which James is silenced, as if he could no longer speak, could no longer sustain the accents and tone that the terms of the correspondence assume. And, following in the wake of the ninth and tenth letters, the Russian's cheerful report gathers a certain irony; for it suggests that now only an outsider can respond to America with unalloyed affirmation, and that James himself has come to a far deeper and more painful perception.

The movement of James toward disillusionment and alienation that Letter IX had signaled reaches its culmination in Letter XII. Here, with an abruptness that resembles the incoherence of hysteria, he renounces all attempts to pursue the plan of the correspondence: the leisurely accumulation of information and interpretation breaks down utterly and is replaced by an impassioned cry of anguish and confusion. The letter becomes one long dramatic monologue, mirroring in the violence of its language and the convolutions of its thought the state of psychic shock to which James is reduced by the collapse of his world. The war is upon him, and the prosperity and order on which his happiness depended are shattered. The dark vision that Charleston had induced has now become the reality of his daily life; the murderous hostility of the snakes has overtaken mankind.

Exposed to the raids of the British and their Indian allies, the farm has been transformed into a place of torment:

> We never sit down, either to dinner or supper, but the least noise immediately spreads a general alarm, and prevents us from enjoying the comfort of our meals. The very appetite, proceeding from labour and peace of mind, is gone: we eat just enough to keep us alive: our sleep is disturbed by the most frightful dreams: sometimes I start awake, as if the great hour of danger was come; at other times the howling of our dogs seems to announce the arrival of our enemy; we leap out of bed and run to arms: my poor wife, with panting bosom and silent tears, takes leave of me, as if we were to see each other no more; she snatches the youngest children from their beds, who, suddenly awakened, increase by their innocent questions, the horror of the dreadful moment. She tries to hide them in the cellar, as if our cellar was inaccessible to the fire. (273)

All has changed: his wife and children, once the center of his joys and hopes, are now an intolerable burden of anxiety for James; the mild and beneficent government of Britain now wields the torch and the scalping knife; the harmonious and tolerant community, torn now by the tensions of war, seethes with suspicion and accusation. And with the change, the despair and negation of James's Charleston meditations return to overwhelm him:

> When . . . I contemplate my situation, and the thousand streams of evil with which I am surrounded, . . . I am convulsed—convulsed sometimes to that degree as to be tempted to exclaim—Why has the Master of the world permitted so much indiscriminate evil throughout every part of this poor planet, at all times, and among all kinds of people? It ought surely to be the punishment of the wicked only. I bring that cup to my lips, of which I must soon taste, and shudder at its bitterness. What then is life, I ask myself, is it a gracious gift? No, it is too bitter; a gift means something valuable conferred, but life appears to be a mere accident, and of the worst kind: we are born to be victims of diseases and passions, of mischances and death: better not to be than to be miserable.—Thus, impiously I roam, I fly from one erratic thought to another, and my mind, irritated by these acrimonious reflections, is ready sometimes to lead me to dangerous extremes of violence. (286–87)

The first half of Letter XII thus seems to enact that period of paralysis which is James's first response to the shock of experience and during which he is swept by wave after wave of agonized thought, thought which points to the final negation of suicide as its inevitable outcome. But, midway in the letter, the stasis of will breaks; and he announces his choice of the course that he will pursue.

The nature of that choice had been anticipated in Letter IX, where James had concluded his gloomy survey of the globe with a comparison of primitive society and civilization; although both are dominated by evil, he gives his preference to the former, for its poverty and simplicity inhibit the growth of corruption: there "real evil is more scarce, more supportable, and less enormous" (232). Now he is prepared to act on that preference, to abandon his farm and community and to "revert into a state approaching nearer to that of nature" (289) by transporting his family to the village of a remote Indian tribe with which he had traded in his youth. Desperately, he musters every conceivable bit of support for his decision. Reminding himself that white captives often refuse to be repatriated and that Indians habitually resist the lures of white civilization, he believes that the savage way of life must offer "something more congenial to our native dispositions than the fictitious society in which we live" (295).

But James is not impelled toward the wigwam by the lure of the primitive. Without membership in some society, he realizes, life is physically insupportable and psychically unendurable. The Indian community, sufficient "to answer all the primary wants of man, and to constitute him a social being" (289), is the only one available to him. That his is a most desperate choice—one forced upon him and not embraced in a romantic passion for savagery—is made clear by the plans he forms to immunize his family from all that is most characteristic of the Indian way of life. He dreads "lest the imperceptible charm of Indian education may seise" his children, and hopes that, by training them to agriculture rather than hunting, he can prevent them from "becoming wild; it is the chase and the food it procures that have this strange effect" (304). He hopes that his wife and daughter will not succumb to the "savage customs" of personal adornment (305) and is thankful that his daughter's suitor will accompany them; "for however I respect the simple, the inoffensive, society of these people in their villages, the strongest prejudices would make me abhor any alliance with them in blood: disagreeable, no doubt, to nature's intentions, which have strongly divided us by so many indelible characters" (308). He will do his best to instill the profit motive in his children and teach them to venerate property, so that they will not sink into the idleness and apathy of their neighbors. Safe in their little enclave of agrarianism and acquisitiveness, James and his family will try to survive as parasites on the Indian community, rather than as participants in it.

In a very real sense, this decision to abandon the farmhouse for the wigwam is a substitute for suicide, a desperate means of purchasing peace, as James's final justification of his scheme suggests: "My heart, sometimes, seems tired with beating, it wants rest like my eye-lids, which feel oppressed with so many watchings" (309). With good reason, James contemplates "this proposed metamorphosis" (313) with regret. It is the repudiation of all the bright assurance that animates the first two-thirds of the book, an abandonment of the very bases of his own serene existence and a denial of his vision of America as the asylum of the oppressed and the mother of a new and happier race.

If the European immigrant became a new man on reaching the shores of America, the American, James, now moves in the direction of the oldest man of all, the man of the woods. And yet, ironically, James's decision is consistent with his earlier views. The answer to trouble is still movement and metamorphosis; in the face of misery, one picks up and moves on, leaving the old worries and troubles behind and contriving a new identity. But the hysterical tension of Letter XII, the frantic attempts at self-persuasion, and the manifest instability of the solution that James there proposes—all seem to indicate that the process has reached the end of its line and that the ending is failure.

James's story, then, is one of disillusionment. It is strange that the *Letters* should be celebrated as the first full enunciation of the American dream, and not also as a searching criticism of it. For Crèvecoeur's art *is* art; its concern, finally, is not with idyllic dreams alone, but with experience, the field on which dream and reality touch and clash. And it is an American art, for his book carries forward the themes which William Bradford's *Of Plymouth Plantation*, the first great work of a distinctively American imagination, had set in motion one hundred and fifty years before. Like Bradford's book, the *Letters* follows the downward arc of the dream gone sour, of a promised land which is discovered to be no haven from history and change, of a chosen people who are found to have no exemption from the follies and sins of mankind at large.

In the figure and fate of James, moreover, can be traced the outlines of the myth of the American Adam as R. W. B. Lewis has defined it; for the pattern of James's experience foreshadows with remarkable precision "the traditional career from bright expectancy to the destruction which, in American literature, has been its perennial reward."[11] If the *Letters* may be regarded as a novel in embryo, then the central action of the book, the basis of its unity and ultimate meaning, is firmly rooted not in the American dream but in an American myth, one which, unlike the dream, contains the possibility of tragedy.

III *Anecdote and Confession*

The epistolary narrative of the *Letters*, embracing, as it does, the entire book, is the primary source of its structural unity. Within that enclosing form, however, Crèvecoeur employs a variety of smaller forms, some incidentally and others so habitually that their repetition becomes in itself a unifying device. Occasionally a single form encompasses a whole letter or, in the Nantucket and Martha's Vineyard series, a group of letters. More often, several forms appear within an individual letter, either in sequence or so intermingled and overlaid as to operate virtually simultaneously. The simplest of these formal modes, the conventional expository essay, is also technically the least successful in Crèvecoeur's hands.

In approach and content, Crèvecoeur's exposition may be chiefly reportorial, as it is in the five letters on the whaling islands, packed with objective detail but bearing a minimum of commentary; or it may be primarily analytical, as it is in the first half of Letter III and in the opening paragraphs of Letter IX, where a few facts are made to carry a heavy burden of interpretation and theory. Whether reportorial or analytical, the expository passages of the *Letters* suffer from Crèvecoeur's indifference to the principles of logical organization. Confused by arbitrary paragraphing, sidetracked by digressive excursions, worried by contradictions and battered by repetitions, the reader is often sustained only by the inherent interest of the substance and by the charm and vigor of the prose style.

When Crèvecoeur descends from the lofty perspective of exposition and adopts the more colloquial tone of anecdotal narration, he gains immensely in economy and coherence. Brief anecdotes are scattered throughout the *Letters*. Some of them, like the little story in Letter III of the cooperative banquet in the wilderness, serve no expository function; rather, they are offered for their piquant flavor and as characteristic episodes in the experience of James. More commonly, the anecdote begins as evidence in support of some expository point but then develops to the extent that it gathers an interest of its own. For example, James pauses in the course of his remarks on the frugality and simplicity of the inhabitants of Nantucket to supply an illustration:

A few years ago, two *single-horse chairs* were imported from Boston, to the great offense of these prudent citizens; nothing appeared to them more culpable than the use of such gaudy painted vehicles, in contempt of the more useful and more simple *single-horse carts* of their fathers. This piece of extravagant and unknown luxury almost caused a schism, and set every tongue a-going; some predicted the approaching ruin of those families that had imported them; others feared the dangers of example: never, since the foundation of the town, had there happened any thing which so much alarmed this primitive community. One of the possessors of these profane chairs, filled with repentance, wisely sent it back to the continent; the other, more obstinate and perverse, in defiance of all remonstrances, persisted in the use of his chair until by degrees they became more reconciled to it; though I observed that the wealthiest and the most respectable people still go to meeting or to their farms in a *single-horse cart* with a decent awning fixed over it. . . . (195)

The point is made, but along the way the passage develops a narrative shape that is complete and satisfying in itself, beginning with the introduction of the disturbing element, lingering over the spreading conflict, and ending with the restoration of calm and the triumph of the old ways. The tone of this account of a crisis brought on by a pair of one-horse shays is also skillfully managed. The diction effectively carries the attitude of mock-seriousness on which the passage is constructed, at once pumping up the proportions of the conflict with language suggestive of religious controversy and the outrage of heresy (*schism, profane, repentance*) and reminding the reader of its true scale with the tart homeliness of *set every tongue a-going*. Viewed in its context, the anecdote wryly qualifies the respectful and admiring stance that the passages of straightforward exposition take toward the sandy utopia of the whalemen.

The longest of the anecdotes in the *Letters*, the "History of Andrew, the Hebridean" in Letter III, is more loosely constructed than the best of the brief ones, but it sustains throughout the several episodes of which it is composed a unified theme and consistent tone. Offered as an illustration of the process by which the European becomes the American, the new man, the history of Andrew is a story of unalloyed success, a small duplication of the pattern traced by Franklin's *Autobiography*. But Andrew's success, unlike Franklin's, is less the result of his own shrewdness and energy than of the new conditions in which he finds himself; he is swept to success by the economic opportunity and social mobility which the American environment affords him. Like James, Andrew is, in an important sense, the creature of his surroundings, and the rising movement of his career serves as an ironic foil to James's descent from security to chaos.

The tale of Andrew is not only a representative of the American success story: it is an early example of that mainstay of the American popular tale, the greenhorn's misadventures. Accustomed to the austere and circumscribed life of the barren little island of Barra from which he comes, Andrew responds to the strange ways of the New World with naïve amazement. At his first sight of "several large Lancaster six-horse waggons" (better known today by the town of their manufacture, Conestoga), he wonders "what was the use of these great moving houses, and where those big horses came from" (96). Having never wielded an ax or ridden a horse, he must be carefully trained in the techniques of frontier farming, but no amount of schooling can prepare him for every possibility. One Sabbath his employer, Mr. P. R., goes to meeting and leaves him in charge of the house. As Andrew is diligently reading his Bible, nine painted Indians suddenly appear on the piazza. Barring the door as securely as he can, he rushes upstairs to get the sword which he had brought with him from Barra. The Indians force the door open and begin to dine on Mr. P. R.'s store of food:

> At this instant, Andrew, with his broad sword in his hand, entered the room; the Indians earnestly looking at him, and attentively watching his motions. After a very few reflections, Andrew found that his weapon was useless, when opposed to nine tomahawks, but this did not diminish his anger; on the contrary, it grew greater, on observing the calm impudence with which they were devouring the family-provisions. Unable to resist, he called them names in broad Scotch, and ordered them to desist and be gone; to which the Indians (as they told me afterwards) replied in their equally broad idiom. It must have been a most unintelligible altercation between this honest Barra man and nine Indians who did not much care for any thing he could say. At last he ventured to lay his hands on one of them, in order to turn him out of the house. Here Andrew's fidelity got the better of his prudence; for

the Indian, by his motions, threatened to scalp him, while the rest gave the war-whoop. This horrid noise so effectually frightened poor Andrew, that, unmindful of his courage, of his broad sword, and his intentions, he rushed out, left them masters of the house, and disappeared. (103–4)

But the Indians are old friends of Mr. P. R.; and, on Andrew's return to the house, they enjoy a good laugh and invite him to puff their calumets in token of their amity.

Again, the shape and pace of the anecdote are indicative of the skillful story-teller. The selection of detail and the phrasing are artfully designed to exploit the comic possibilities generated by the collision of the two cultures and by the misguided heroism of the novice. Indeed, Crèvecoeur's sense of humor was paid the tribute of plagiarism by Enos Hitchcock, who appropriated the story of the encounter of Andrew and the Indians, along with other materials from the *Letters,* for his didactic novel *The Farmer's Friend* (1793).[12] But, if the immediate value of the episode lies in its broad comedy, it nevertheless functions rather grimly within the total context of the book; for, like the history of Andrew as a whole, it serves as counterpoint to the experience of James. The contrast between the Indians, who play their practical joke on Andrew, and those for whom James listens with fearful anxiety in Letter XII is a measure of the distance between a world of benign illusion and a world of terrifying reality.

The dominant mode of two of the most important letters, the second and the twelfth, is neither exposition nor narrative but a form of expression that resembles more closely than anything else certain phases of the eighteenth-century sentimental novel or journal of sensibility. Perhaps it might be best labeled "the confession," for in it the speaker, adopting a tone of extreme intimacy, lays bare his inmost hopes and fears. Like the lyric poem, the confession is constructed upon the speaker's revelation of a state of mind. Its focus is subjective and introspective; its interest derives from the play of thought and feeling more than from the external objects and events to which the speaker responds. As befits its perspective of recollection, the mood of Letter II is serene, if sentimental. We see the farmer of feelings cultivating his crop of tender reminiscences and gathering his harvest of tears and smiles.

Although James regrets that "I can feel much more than I am able to express" and "cannot describe the various emotions of love, of gratitude, of conscious pride, which thrill in my heart and often overflow in involuntary tears" (24, 25), he nevertheless manages to convey a sufficient portion of his feelings. We share in his moments of paternal ecstasy and in the pleasing emotions of homecoming; we are penetrated by wonder as he contemplates the transformation of an egg into a fowl or observes the instinctual sagacity of his cattle. As James assures us, "with candour, though with diffidence, I endeavour to follow the thread of my feelings" (26).

The confessional note is sounded still more strongly in Letter XII, which, as a recital of James's "distresses," is precisely balanced against the account of his "pleasures" in Letter II. But in this last letter, the tone takes on an urgency and immediacy foreign to the dreamy mood of Letter II. The items of James's concern are not leisurely fished from the meandering stream of memory but are forced upon his consciousness by the pressure of his present experience. In the manner of a dramatic monologue, the letter becomes the enactment of a state of mind rather than simply a statement of it; for the very tone and movement of the discourse suggest the wild gestures of hysteria. Appropriately, the relation which James here seeks to establish between himself and his correspondent is the closest and most confiding of any of the letters. Aware of the difference between his own desperate situation and that of Mr. F. B., safe and prosperous in London, he pleads for a sympathetic tear and asks pardon for the display of misery that he has thrust upon his correspondent; "my repetitions, my wild, my trifling, reflections, they proceed from the agitations of my mind and the fulness of my heart; the action of thus retracing them seems to lighten the burthen, and to exhilarate my spirits" (297). As gesture, as plea, as catharsis, Letter XII marks the moment at which the submerged plot of the book breaks to the surface, and the language itself becomes action.

IV *Symbol and Fable*

For all their appropriateness to the design of the *Letters* and the considerable skill with which they are written, Crèvecoeur's confessional passages are apt to annoy the modern reader because of their heavy reliance on sentimental conventions that no longer seem viable. The acute self-consciousness of the speaker makes him seem to be posturing before a mirror, egotistically absorbed in the effect of the reflected image. We have ceased to admire the character who delights in pointing to his own capacity for weeping and for wonder. Far more congenial to the modern taste is the form which seems most characteristic of Crèvecoeur's art, the symbolic scene. Here everything is done by indirection; indeed, the method is so unobtrusive that the inattentive reader may easily take the scenes at face value, accepting them simply as passages of factual description.

The non-literal quality of Crèvecoeur's descriptive passages is most apparent in the conclusion of Letter IX, in much of Letter II, and everywhere in Letter X. In nearly every instance the scene springs from what purports to be direct observation of nature, and almost invariably the content of that observation can be demonstrated to be derived from a source other than Crèvecoeur's own experience. The celebrated description of the hummingbird in Letter X can serve as an example. This passage, which D. H. Lawrence praised for its "primal, dark veracity,"[13] derives most of its essential elements from Raynal's *Histoire philosophique*. Raynal gives the following account of the bird:

Its beak is long, and pointed like a needle. . . .
The humming bird lives entirely on the juice of flowers, fluttering from one to another, like the bees. Sometimes it buries itself in the calix of the largest flowers. . . . When it is tired, it lights upon the nearest tree or stake; rests a few minutes, and flies again to the flowers. Notwithstanding its weakness, it does not appear timid; but will suffer a man to approach within eight or ten feet of it.
Who could imagine, that so diminutive an animal could be malicious, passionate and quarelsome? They are often seen fighting together with great fury and obstinacy. . . .
These little birds are all impatience. When they come near a flower, if they find it faded and withered, they tear all the leaves asunder. The precipitation, with which they peck it, betrays, it is said, the rage with which they are animated. Towards the end of the summer, thousands of flowers may be seen stript of all their leaves by the fury of the fly-birds.[14]

The "insect bird" of the *Letters* is remarkably similar:

> Its bill is as long and as sharp as a coarse sewing needle; like the
> bee, nature has taught it to find out in the calix of flowers and
> blossoms, those mellifluous particles that serve it for sufficient
> food. . . . [S]ometimes, from what motives I know not, it will
> tear and lacerate flowers into a hundred pieces, for, strange to
> tell, they are the most irascible of the feathered tribe.–Where do
> passions find room in so diminutive a body?– They often fight
> with the fury of lions, until one of the combatants falls a sacrifice
> and dies. When fatigued, it has often perched within a few feet
> of me, and on such favourable opportunities, I have surveyed it
> with the most minute attention. (242–43)

The differences between the two passages—the more effective
ordering of Crèvecoeur's description, his injection of a superintending Nature, and his heightening of the attitude of wonder—
testify to the artistic tact of the *Letters;* but they do not obscure
the fact that Crèvecoeur was indebted to Raynal both for his
facts and for his leading idea—the paradoxical union of littleness
and ferocity. Clearly Lawrence, who had "read about hummingbirds elsewhere, in Bates and W. H. Hudson, for example," but
for whom it was "left to the American Farmer to show . . . the
real little raging lion,"[15] was unacquainted with Raynal.

The majority of James's natural descriptions have a source
closer to home: indigenous animal folklore and tall tales. Nearly
every commentator on Crèvecoeur has raised a suspicious eye-
brow over the account in Letter II of James's rescue of fifty-four
living bees from the craw of a kingbird, but until fairly recently
the veracity of the other items in James's natural history has gone
unchallenged. In 1939, however, James R. Masterson published a
conclusive demonstration of the folkloristic basis of one of the
anecdotes in Letter X, a recital of the fatal career of a pair of
leather boots in which the fangs of a rattlesnake have become
embedded; the story would seem to have originated in a report
to the Royal Society in 1714 and still survives in Texas as an oral
tale of a venomous automobile tire.[16] In another article, the same
author has identified the descriptions of snakes fascinating their
prey and of the startling effects of the bite of the copperhead, also
in Letter X, as additional evidence of Crèvecoeur's use of folk

materials.[17] Laurence M. Klauber's recent and definitive study of rattlesnakes supports Masterson's findings by pointing out the zoological improbability of these three bits of snake-lore and casts doubt, moreover, on accounts of battles between snakes of different species and stories of snakes so thoroughly domesticated that they come when called, both also represented in Letter X.[18]

There seems little question that much of the information on birds and insects in Letter II is as dubious as the unnatural history of Letter X. Surely the yellow wasps that build their underground homes in the meadows of James's farm are a hazard to mowers, but are the hornets of Pennsylvania so susceptible to kind treatment that they can be encouraged to nest in the parlor and to catch flies "even on the eyelids of my children" (42)? Is it true that all the quail of America are descended from those that dwelt on the farm of a kind citizen of Connecticut, who, during a particularly severe winter, fed the birds and enabled them to survive a season that killed the rest of their species?

Whatever the demands that he makes on the reader's credulity, James preserves the straight face that is the mark of the expert liar: "believe me, what I write is all true and real" (40). But James is a liar only if one conceives of him as a vehicle of information about America. Viewed as a fictional character, an actor in an imaginary landscape, he speaks the truth; for the reality of the book is the world which he experiences and reports. That world differs from the actual one not only in the bizarre behavior of its animals but in the extraordinary relevance of the life of its nature to the life of man. Indeed, one can formulate a principle: the more drastic the departure of the materials of the *Letters* from the known facts of Crèvecoeur's life or from the beings and processes of the actual world, the more likely it is that those materials are invested with symbolic significance.

The symbolic materials of the *Letters* are not fragmentary and unrelated; rather, they are assembled within the individual letter to form an integrated system of implied meanings, a system that combines with the stated meanings to develop the over-all theme of the letter. Letter II offers a particularly intricate example of the method. As has been seen, the function of the letter is to convey an impression of the texture and feel of the daily life of the American Farmer and to define the norm of James's past experience. But, in the course of the operation of his farm and the management of his family, James is confronted again and again with the problem of government. The farm becomes a microcosmic political unit; within that sphere he is the ruler, and his family and his livestock are his subjects. His problem is the perennial one of all governors: the achievement of that delicate balance between freedom and authority in which the pursuit of private goals does not degenerate into anarchic competition and in which the maintenance of social order does not become a cruel and stifling oppression.

Accordingly, he exerts his paternal authority over his children with great mildness: "I have to contrive little punishments for their little faults, small encouragements for their good actions, and a variety of other expedients dictated by various occasions" (44). His horses and cows require a harsher discipline, for the stronger animals "always strive to encroach on their neighbours. Unsatisfied with their portion, they eagerly swallow it in order to have an opportunity of taking what is given to others, except they are prevented. Some I chide; others, unmindful of my admonitions, receive some blows" (31).

But even the beasts of the stable respond to gentle treatment, for "my well-known voice has immediate influence; and soon restores peace and tranquillity." James's government of his cattle offers a clear analogy to the government of human societies. The passions of the animals "are exactly the same as among men. The law is to us precisely what I am in my barnyard, a bridle and check to prevent the strong and greedy from oppressing the timid and weak. . . . Thus," he observes, "by superior knowledge, I govern all my cattle as wise men are obliged to govern fools and the ignorant" (31-32).

As the letter proceeds, multiplying its examples of James's beneficent intervention in the affairs not only of his domestic animals but of the wild creatures as well, it becomes more and more apparent that he is enacting a parable for governors. In a role that is analogous to that of a benevolent monarch or even to that of the watchful God, he curbs the powerful and succors the weak. He refuses to take advantage of the winter-starved quail that enter his barn in search of food; instead, he gives them grain and spreads chaff to prevent their tender feet from freezing to the

[97]

earth. He removes the box of a wren which had usurped its neighbor's property to prevent a repetition of the crime. He consigns the wasps which sting him as he mows to a hell of fire and brimstone, thinking it "a great pity" to be "obliged to execute this dreadful sentence in my own defence" (43); but he takes satisfaction in having redeemed the fly-catching hornets: "though they are fierce and vindictive, yet kindness and hospitality have made them useful and harmless" (42).

We are apt to remember those hornets when James in later letters tells us of the savage violence to which maltreated Negroes and Indians are driven by their white exploiters. Indeed, the animal life of James's farm anticipates in many ways what we are later to learn of the society and government of America. As D. H. Lawrence noted, the story of the rescue of the bees from the belly of the kingbird is "a parable of the American resurrection" from "the craw of the king-bird of Europe,"[19] the subject of Letter III. James's bees, like American settlers, develop an abhorrence of restraint, preferring the rough habitation of a hollow tree in the woods "to the best polished mahogany hive." But James, wise governor that he is, indulges their appetite for liberty: "I seldom thwart their inclinations. It is in freedom that they work. Were I to confine them, they would dwindle away and quit their labour" (33). Let Parliament take heed.

If the animals of James's farm behave in odd ways, then, it is because they are often doing duty as characters in a fable. That fable of government by and large supports the mood of serenity that prevails in Letter II. Surely the microcosmic farm is disturbed by quarrels and wrangles, injustices and hardships; but just as surely it is superintended by the alert and kindly James. Whether one limits the application of the fable to the American political system as it is described in Letter III and in the series on Nantucket and Martha's Vineyard, or sees in it a larger symbolic image of God's providential government of the universe, an extension that Crèvecoeur's diction and imagery sometimes seem to warrant, its import is reassuring. In time all wrongs are righted; all suffering relieved. But, when Crèvecoeur turns to the natural world outside the context of the fable, jarring contradictions and unsettling implications intrude and make the reign of order and freedom seem something less than inevitable.

For James, the natural sphere is not only a reflection of the world of man but an ideal, a perfect state of harmonious order by which the extent of man's confusion and error can be gauged. That view is authorized by his stated belief in instinct as an infallible regulatory agency, as the direct expression in nature of the divine plan. James is astonished by the behavior of "those animals, which have long been tenants of my farm. . . : some of them seem to surpass even men in memory and sagacity. . . . What then is this instinct which we so debase, and of which we are taught to entertain so diminutive an idea?" (28). The more he studies the problem, the more convinced he is of the superiority of natural instinct over human reason:

> [T]he whole oeconomy, of what we proudly call the brute creation, is admirable in every circumstance; and vain man, though adorned with the additional gift of reason, might learn, from the perfection of instinct, how to regulate the follies, and how to temper the errors, which this second gift often makes him commit. This is a subject on which I have often bestowed the most serious thoughts. I have often blushed within myself, and been greatly astonished, when I have compared the unerring path they all follow, all just, all proper, all wise, up to the necessary degree of perfection, with the coarse, the imperfect, systems of men, not merely as governors and kings, but as masters, as husbands, as fathers, as citizens. But this is a sanctuary in which an ignorant farmer must not presume to enter. (39)

This passage marks the farthest flight of James's optimism. It contains the implication that, with instinct firmly in the seat, the need for any form of external government, whether by human political agencies or by the providential hand of God, disappears; instinct alone provides an automatic and perfect order. Acting on that assumption, James attempts to found his own life on the rock of instinct; deliberately shunning the lure of reason, he grounds his values and his pleasures on those simple routines that most closely approximate the pattern of animal existence.

But he cannot have it both ways: nature cannot function both as a mirror of the human world and as an ideal for man to emulate. The specific examples of animal behavior from which the fable of government is constructed have furnished too many instances of rapacity and cruelty to allow one to share James's belief in the perfection of instinct. The wren that plunders its neighbor's nest forces him to acknowledge the contradiction: "Where did this little bird learn that spirit of injustice? It was not endowed with what we term reason! Here then is a proof that both those gifts border very near on one another, for we see the perfection of the one mixing with the errors of the other" (41).

More importantly, the contradiction calls attention to the fallibility of James's theoretical constructs. If his own evidence undermines his conception of the utopian reign of instinct, can one trust any more securely in the benign operations of an external authority, the basis of the fable of government? At one point in Letter II, James makes a passing observation that would seem to expose the unreality of any vision of perfect harmony. In the tone of open-eyed wonder that is the keynote of the letter, he confesses that "I am astonished to see that nothing exists but what has its enemy; one species pursues and lives upon the other" (28). That momentary insight into the predatory reality that his dreams of harmony obscure is confirmed and extended in subsequent letters. For the time being, it lies dormant, an unexamined portent of the drastically altered view of nature that is to come.

In the chapters that immediately follow Letter II, animal imagery appears infrequently, chiefly in the form of similes which, though inconsequential in themselves, help to keep before the reader the links between the human world and the world of birds and insects that Letter II has forged. Thus James, contrasting the exalted concerns of the historian with his own humble ones, remarks that "eagles soar high—I, a feebler bird, cheerfully content myself with skipping from bush to bush, and living on insignificant insects" (87). If James is a predator, he is no more threatening than a songbird.

But the few direct references to animals in these letters focus on images of hunting and of being hunted. The backwoodsmen of Letter III exist "in a perfect state of war; that of man against man . . . ; that of man against every wild inhabitant of these venerable woods, of which they are come to dispossess them. There men appear to be no better than carnivorous animals, of a superior rank" (55). They are infected by the wildness around them: "The deer often come to eat their grain, the wolves to destroy their sheep, the bears to kill their hogs, the foxes to catch their poultry. This surrounding hostility immediately puts the gun into their hands" (63), and "the worst of them" degenerate "altogether into the hunting state" (65-66). No less predatory are the seamen of the whaling islands, as James's vivid description of the whale hunt in Letter VI makes clear. But the backwoods and Nantucket are exceptions to the norm of American life; they are the fringe of violence that surrounds the peaceful agrarian center.

In the appalling tableau of the caged Negro at the end of Letter IX, the animal imagery of Letter II returns. But if wolves and whales give way once more to birds and insects, there is no return to the charming little fable in which man succors the helpless animals and leads them into the path of virtue. In this startling emblem of the world as torture chamber, the birds and insects become winged furies, embodiments of all the forces of destruction and savage cruelty, both natural and human, that now dominate James's vision of the universe. The branches of the tree from which the Negro is suspended are "covered with large birds of prey, fluttering about, and anxiously endeavouring to perch on the cage" (233).

Acting now in a world in which man and nature are enemies, James intervenes by firing at the birds, which retreat a short distance, making "a most hideous noise." But the intervention, unlike those of Letter II, comes too late to save the Negro: "the birds had already picked out his eyes; his cheek-bones were bare; his arms had been attacked in several places, and his body seemed covered with a multitude of wounds." And, although the birds move off at the sound of James's gun, they are immediately replaced by new tormentors, the swarms of insects that cover the body of the sufferer, "eager to feed on his mangled flesh and to drink his blood" (233-34).

Marius Bewley detects a "faint but terrible sacramental echo" in that last phrase,[20] but the more immediate association is one which Crèvecoeur's own writings establish. Throughout his books, from the *Letters* to the *Voyage,* the utmost horror which his imagination can picture is the consumption of human flesh. The idea of the carnivore is always intensely repellent to him; that revulsion underlies James's condemnation of the predatory backwoodsman and his fear of the Indian way of life. More than any of the theories of the Physiocrats, it is the source of his fervent advocacy of agriculture; for farming redeems man from the bloody hunt and rescues him from the atavistic degeneration that is a consequence of the eating of wild meat. The depth of James's distress in Letter XII is indicated by his comparison of the British marauders to "the lions of Africa," transported to the peaceful fields of America and released to "kill us in order to prey upon our carcasses" (283).

In Crèvecoeur's imagination, it is but one step from meat-eating to man-eating: the members of a hunting society will, in time of famine, hunt each other; the wolf that feeds on sheep becomes the lion that preys upon man. Thus in all his writings the act of devouring human flesh, for him the ultimate violence, functions as his most intense symbol of evil. In Letter IX, then, the birds and insects which James had formerly regulated with benevolent firmness become the agents of an uncontrollable violence, the symbolic image of all the tormenting evils of the human condition. In that transformation, the disintegration of James's whole world is epitomized. The idyll of order is gone forever; the destructiveness and hostility which James had held in check now overrun mankind; and the last words which James hears from the multilated lips of the Negro convey the full horror of the change: "the birds, the birds; aaah me!"

In the wake of this transformation, the animal imagery of Letter X, "On Snakes; and on the Humming-Bird," takes on a sinister significance. The method of the letter is less susceptible to analysis than that of Letter II, for here the several passages of the natural description are not contained within the neat pattern of a fable, nor are they supported by any general narrative framework. Rather, the letter consists of an apparently random collection of observations and anecdotes, all of which, with the exception of the account of the hummingbird, deal with the snakes of Eastern America.

James draws no helpful analogies between the spheres of men and animals, nor does he interpret in any other way the phenomena which he records. Everything is implied; all that we are given directly is the natural fact and an indication of James's emotional response to it. Thus James makes no reference to the traditional Satanic associations of snakes. He must not, for on its deepest level the letter itself is the dramatic enactment of the temptation of James by the lure of wildness, the beauty of violence.

The creatures that James describes at the opening of the letter are recognizably dangerous. For the poison of the copperhead, "no remedy has yet been discovered. . . . Let man beware of it" (236). The victim of the copperhead undergoes a ghastly metamorphosis: "The poor wretch instantly swelled in a most dreadful manner; a multitude of spots of different hues alternately appeared and vanished on different parts of his body: his eyes were filled with madness and rage; he cast them on all present with the most vindictive looks; he thrust out his tongue as the snakes do; he hissed through his teeth with inconceivable strength, and became an object of terror to all by-standers" (236-37).

The relation between man and animal that is hereby established at the outset of the letter is not one of analogy or simile; here man *becomes* the animal, becomes, indeed, the writhing embodiment of furious malice. The rattler, the only other venomous snake of the region, is less of a menace. Several antidotes for its poison are known; moreover, rattlers "are extremely inactive, and, if not touched, are perfectly inoffensive." The Indians "often regale on them," for "their flesh is extremely sweet and white" (237, 238), a fact that is not disturbing unless we recall James's settled conviction that "Eating of wild meat alters . . . [man's] temper" (65). So tractable is the rattler that it can be made a pet, coming when called and turning on its back to be stroked with a soft brush "as a cat does before the fire" (238).

Yet for all this docility, a rattler was the cause, as has been noted, of a most deplorable accident to a Dutch family of Minisink in New York. While mowing in his field, the father was struck on his boot by the snake, but without apparent harm. That night, soon after he had pulled off his boots, the farmer was stricken with a strange illness and died. A few days later, his son, who had inherited the boots, died in precisely the same way. The solution of the mystery was not discovered until a neighbor, the purchaser of the deadly boots, also was stricken; the physician who was summoned to his aid guessed the cause of the malady and saved his patient by administering the appropriate antidote. The boots were examined, and embedded in the leather were the fangs, positioned so as to scratch the wearer's skin when the boot was drawn off. All dangers, it would seem, are not easily recognized.

The central object of James's attention in the letter is neither the copperhead nor the rattler but the harmless black snake, "remarkable for nothing but its industry, agility, beauty, and the art of inticing birds by the power of its eyes. I admire it much, and never kill it" (236). In the context of the letter, James's remark that the black snake "always diverts me, because it excites no idea of danger" (240), sounds ominous overtones. He is intrigued by the ability of the snake to hypnotize its victims:

> On some occasions, they present themselves half in the reptile state, half erect. Their eyes and their heads, in the erect posture, appear to great advantage: the former display a fire which I have often admired, and it is by these they are enabled to fascinate birds and squirrels. When they have fixed their eyes on an animal, they become immovable, only turning their head sometimes to the right and sometimes to the left, but still with their sight invariably directed to the object. The distracted victim, instead of flying its enemy, seems to be arrested by some invincible power; it screems; now approaches, and then recedes; and, after skipping about with unaccountable agitation, finally rushes into the jaws of the snake, and is swallowed, as soon as it is covered with a slime or glue to make it slide easily down the throat of the devourer. (240–41)

James's repeated emphasis throughout the letter on the fiery eyes of the black snake and on his own admiration of them suggests that he too feels their "invincible power" and succumbs to it. He is transfixed by the spectacle of the combat of a six-foot black snake and a water snake:

> [I]n the fury of their first encounter, they appeared in an instant firmly twisted together; and, whilst their united tails beat the ground, they mutually tried with open jaws to lacerate each other. What a fell aspect did they present! their heads were compressed to a very small size, their eyes flashed fire; and, after this conflict had lasted about five minutes, the second found means to disengage itself from the first, and hurried toward the ditch. Its antagonist instantly assumed a new posture; and, half creeping and half erect, with a majestic mien, overtook and attacked the

other again, which placed itself in the same attitude and prepared to resist. The scene was uncommon and beautiful; for thus opposed, they fought with their jaws, biting each other with the utmost rage. . . . (244)

For James, violence has become a mode of beauty. By the moral standards that have prevailed throughout the earlier letters, his passionate admiration of naked power and of animosity constitutes an assent, a capitulation to the forces of destruction.

The battle of the snakes is the last instance of extended animal imagery in the *Letters*. The force of that imagery, however, extends through the concluding letter of the book. The natural world which the book has pictured, a world which begins as a peaceable kingdom and ends as a jungle of hostility, serves to illuminate and intensify the story of James as it reaches its catastrophic conclusion in Letter XII. There James, as he had in Letter II, turns to the instinctual behavior of animals as a guide for his own actions and a sanction for his motives: "The fox flies or deceives the hounds that pursue him; the bear, when overtaken, boldly resists and attacks them; the hen, the very timid hen, fights for the preservation of her chicken, nor does she decline to attack, and to meet on the wing, even the swift kite. Shall man, then, provided both with instinct and reason, unmoved, unconcerned, and passive, see his subsistence consumed, and his progeny either ravished from him or murdered? Shall fictitious reason extinguish the unerring impulse of instinct?" (285). Like the fox, the bear, and the hen, James is a hunted animal; and he must struggle to preserve himself and his family. The natural world, which had earlier offered models of domestic harmony and communal order, now teaches only the lesson of raw survival.

But the animal imagery casts still darker shadows than these. As Letter X makes clear, Crèvecoeur's figurative uses of nature include reinforcement of the myth which underlies the narrative pattern of the entire work, the Fall of Man. In Letter II, as James superintends the creatures of his farm and exemplifies the principles of wise governance, he strengthens the paradisiac quality of the letter by his idyllic re-enactment of the dominion over the beasts of the field and the fowl of the air that God had given Adam. In Letter X, the serpent enters James's Eden to work his corruption, to induce him to shift his allegiance from order and benevolence to violence and rage. By yielding to the fatal attraction of the snake, James brings upon himself the chaos of Letter XII. On the surface level of the narrative, James is simply the victim of forces outside himself, but on this lowermost level of the book—the plane of myth—James becomes a representative figure, not only of the American Everyman but of archetypal man. The chaos is self-created, the image of his own moral disintegration, and his expulsion from the Eden of his farm is no less the result of an inner failure than was Adam's banishment.

CHAPTER 4

Other English Writings

WHEN *Letters from an American Farmer* first appeared in 1782, the publishers promised that, if the book met with a favorable reception, a second volume of letters, "equally interesting with those now published, may soon be expected." But, in the advertisement to the edition of the following year, they foresaw some delay: since Mr. St. John had accepted "a public employment at New York," it was, "perhaps, doubtful whether he will soon be at leisure to revise his papers and give the world a second collection of the American Farmer's Letters."[1] The doubt was well founded. Although Crèvecoeur found the opportunity to work portions of many of the manuscripts that he had written at Pine Hill into the French editions of the *Letters,* a second gathering of his writings in English did not appear until 1925 when Henri L. Bourdin, Ralph H. Gabriel, and Stanley T. Williams published their edition of *Sketches of Eighteenth Century America.*

Crèvecoeur never explained why he failed to publish a second volume of the English *Letters,* but the reasons can be surmised. In the rush of the few months that he spent in England in 1781, he may well have lacked the time to prepare more than one volume for publication. Moreover, his publishers, as their advertisement indicates, probably delayed the project until the response to the first volume was known. But, by the time that the *Letters* was an established success, Crèvecoeur had resumed his French citizenship and had made contact with the literary circles of Paris. From that point forward, the audience that most concerned him was French, and all his publications, with the exception of a few inconsequential pieces that he submitted anonymously to American newspapers during his term as consul, were addressed to that audience.

Finally, Crèvecoeur surely realized that the manuscript sketches and essays that remained after the materials of the *Letters* were assembled were not publishable without drastic reworking. Some merely repeated the contents of the *Letters*. Others offered a practical and rather critically realistic view of farm life in America that was not in consonance with the idyllic note which the early portions of the *Letters* had sounded and which, in large measure, accounted for the popularity of the book. Still worse, the most powerful of the manuscript sketches presented a bitter indictment of the American Revolution, one that the changes in the times and in his own circumstances had rendered obsolete. Since the writing of these sketches, Crèvecoeur had undergone the misery of imprisonment by the British in New York, had made ties with those elements in France which were most friendly to the cause of the American rebels, and had received an appointment as consul to the victorious new republic. The diplomat of 1783 could not speak in the tones of the farmer of 1778, and there is nothing to indicate that he wished to.

Thus the sketches that Bourdin, Gabriel, and Williams assembled from the papers that Crèvecoeur took with him on his flight from Pine Hill constitute the raw materials of a book rather than a completed work. Whatever shape and finish the *Sketches* has are the work of his editors, not of Crèvecoeur himself. They selected eleven of the nineteen unpublished sketches for inclusion in the volume. Since the sequence of the sketches as they appear in the bound volumes of Crèvecoeur's manuscripts conveys no discernible design, the editors devised their own order, apparently modeling the organization of the book on the general pattern of the *Letters*. Like the twelve *Letters*, the twelve chapters of the *Sketches* begin with the depiction of rural life, move toward generalized sociological and political analysis, and end with a vivid account of the agony brought on by the coming of the Revolution.

But, in order to establish that pattern, the editors were forced to do considerable violence to two of the sketches as they exist in manuscript. They deleted half of one, "Susquehanna," and printed the surviving half under the title "The Wyoming Massacre" (Chapter VIII). Another sketch, "A Snow-Storm," was divided to form two separate chapters, "A Snow-Storm as It Affects the American Farmer" (Chapter I) and "The English and the French before the Revolution" (Chapter VI). Other changes were made in the interest of conciseness and smoothness. The opening paragraphs of several of the sketches were cropped; orthography and punctuation were subjected to wholesale regularization; diction and syntax were altered in some instances.

I *The Many Voices of the* Sketches

In spite of all these changes, *Sketches of Eighteenth Century America* remains a non-book, an anthology of heterogeneous pieces that lacks a controlling form, a coherent point of view, and a unifying theme. There are, for example, tantalizing traces of an epistolary structure like the one that gives the *Letters* its basic order; but the circumstances of the correspondence and even the identity of its participants remain obscure. The book begins in what seems to be the familiar accents of the American Farmer as it describes the cares and satisfactions which winter brings to a rural household. The tone of the speaker is a little more pretentious than the one employed in the *Letters*—he can refer to his own "enlightened mind" and to the "aurum potabile" that is the conscientious farm wife—and is markedly more didactic in its recommendations of the various agricultural techniques that are practices by the model "man of foresight." Nevertheless, the astonished interest in the processes of nature, the high priority assigned to order, and the steady celebration of rural simplicity and domestic joys can all be connected with James of the *Letters*. Only the setting, a Canadian or Mohawk landscape, is unfamiliar.

The opening paragraph of Chapter II, "Ant-Hill Town," introduces a radically different consciousness, that of a certain Mr. P. V., who writes while seated in a Virginian arbor, "a verdant temple" around which "stands a double row of the mellifluous locust, the umbrageous catalpas, and the soft magnolias": " 'Tis a grove of Tempé; 'tis a Druidical temple, in point of gloom, shade, and solitude" (51). The well-traveled Mr. P. V. can make easy comparisons between the landscaping of the estates along the Potomac and "the verdant lawns of England, of Ireland, and Normandy" (51-52). His education has endowed him with a taste for the precious phrase and the exotic allusion:

How often have I viewed with admiration that sublime gradation of objects reaching and filling the whole extent of my perception: from the refulgent luminary to the fainting moon, to the dimmed stars, down to the vocal choir, even to the polygonal cobweb, perpendicularly hung or horizontally suspended,—all bespangled with dew-drops refulgent as the diamond, waving to the raptured eyes! 'Tis not that I would mean to recommend to you the worship of fire in this solar appearance. I am far from believing with the disciples of Zoroaster, that the sun is the true Shekinah of the divine presence, the grand tabernacle, the Keblah where He alone resides. No, but relegated as we are at such a distance from the great Author of all, is not it a consolation to view scenes of this nature, by which we are elevated and permitted in thought to approach nearer to His throne? (56)

As the sketch proceeds, the suspicion grows that we are hearing the voice of an early version of Mr. F. B., James's silent correspondent in the *Letters*. There we were told that Mr. F. B. had visited James's farm in the course of a tour from New Hampshire to South Carolina; here Mr. P. V. relates that a mere two months before his arrival in Virginia he had been ensconced before a cheerful hearth in Massachusetts. But, if he is a prototypical Mr. F. B., he is writing not to James but to a friend at home in England with whom he has been engaged in "a long correspondence" (61). It would seem that at the time this sketch was written, about 1769,[2] Crèvecoeur was experimenting with a variety of epistolary strategies. Perhaps his original conception of a series of letters on America involved a number of correspondents, both native inhabitants and European tourists. More likely, the European voice of this sketch and of the visit to Bartram in the *Letters*, first drafted about 1770, was to have been the sole vehicle of the work. If so, and if the strained elegance of "Ant-Hill Town" was to be maintained throughout, Crèvecoeur's decision to adopt instead the American voice of James was indeed a happy one.

The presence of the American voice in Chapter III, "Reflections on the Manners of the Americans," and in Chapter IV, "Thoughts of an American Farmer on Various Rural Subjects," both written about 1774, is unmistakable. Both sketches employ the perspective of a man who was "bred in the woods" (68), a man whose diction is peppered with the homely terms of the American farmer and forester and whose habitual references are not to Classical myth and Eastern religion but to the daily practices and intimate attitudes of the American settler. The modes of expression are familiar to the reader of the *Letters*: the case history of a representative new man, the anecdote of frontier life, and the vignette of an unlikely natural world in which beavers weep, tree toads forecast rain, and fireflies serve as the woodsman's reading lamp.

The problem posed by these two chapters is largely one of context. The sketch "On the Manners of the Americans," for example, is designed to follow certain "preceding letters" (62) which supply information about religion in the American colonies, presumably "Liberty of Worship," which the editors of the *Sketches* print as Chapter XV of their book, and "What Is an American," which was to become the first half of the third chapter of the *Letters*. It is possible that the essay "On the Manners of the Americans" was once intended to bear the relation to "What Is an American" that the "History of Andrew, the Hebridean" does in the published *Letters*.

Like Andrew, the unnamed settler of the *Sketches* is a new man, a man reshaped by the forces of the American environment and lifted by them from poverty and obscurity to a position of wealth and influence. But, unlike Andrew, this settler is a native American who migrates from the settled Eastern regions to the Western frontier. And, still less like Andrew, his metamorphosis is accompanied by a moral deterioration in which self-reliance becomes mere selfishness and shrewdness becomes cunning. Either as a replacement for the history of Andrew or as a complement to it, "On the Manners of the Americans" might have given Letter III a realistic balance that it lacks. But balance and realism were precisely the qualities which the eventual design of the *Letters* forbade in the opening sections of the book, and Crèvecoeur left the essay out.

The second of these sketches, "Thoughts of an American Farmer on Various Rural Subjects," poses a very different problem of context. Rather than being dependent on preliminary material that is missing, it is altogether too self-contained. Composed of four separate letters and comprising more than a quarter of the total text of the *Sketches*, it is virtually a little book in itself. Indeed, one is tempted to regard it as a preliminary draft of the work that was to become the *Letters*. In the first of the four brief letters, Crèvecoeur artfully reveals the identity of his persona and the circumstances of the correspondence: the writer is a farmer in what would seem to be lower New York. On the farm which he inherited from his "sober and industrious" father, he resides with his sharp-tongued, diligent wife and his young children, who "won't be apt to say that I have not trained them up to the plough, for I fix them on it, even from the breast" (93).

His letters are addressed to a sophisticated Englishman who has stopped at the farmer's house on his way south from New Hampshire and who is now touring in Virginia. The English gentleman has given the farmer an extensive account of European agriculture and requested in return information about farming in America. The farmer has undertaken the present series of letters in response to that request, not, however, without severe misgivings:

> . . . I blush at the task you have imposed on me and at the readiness with which I have accepted it. There is something truly ridiculous in a farmer quitting his plough or his axe, and then flying to his pen. His hands as well as his mind do not seem well calculated for this new employment. . . . My wife herself, who has never seen me handle the pen so much in all my life, helps to confound me; she laughs at my folly. What, then, is it that makes me prosecute this theme? Your positive injunctions, my solemn promise, and the desire that you may be enabled to give your friends in Europe a more certain account of our modes of cultivating the earth, as well as of the great advances we must make, and of the inconveniences we labour under. (84–85)

The passage contains, in miniature, most of the essential content of the introductory chapter of the *Letters,* but there are two crucial differences: here the farmer's task, unlike James's, is restricted to the discussion of agriculture; and this farmer, as well as his readers, lacks the assurance and sanction which the minister's encouraging words give to James. These limitations operate throughout the lengthy sketch, for the farmer holds fast to his assigned topic, the only one on which he feels qualified to speak. In great detail and with obvious authority, he describes the agricultural techniques, the tools, and the marketing procedures which the colonists have evolved in the face of the unique problems posed by the American environment. His prevailing attitude is defensive, for he feels compelled to justify any departure from the model husbandry of England by steady reference to the handicaps under which the American farmer must operate—the severity of the climate, the great number of pests, the remoteness from markets. Steadily, too, he offers those handicaps as reasons for opposing any increase of the taxes imposed on the colonies.

These are plausible concerns for an American farmer to have, but Crèvecoeur has endowed his speaker with qualities that suggest a capacity to make a larger statement than one might expect to encounter in an agricultural handbook or a plea for tax relief. He has a gift for vivid and precise description, a tendency to speculate on the general character of American society, an intense interest in nature, and a compassion that sometimes verges on sentimentality. But his remarks on any subject beyond the practical concerns of agriculture are swiftly checked before they can be developed, or else they intrude without preparation and without relation to the discourse as a whole.

At one point in the sketch, the farmer gives voice to an insight that lies at the very core of Crèvecoeur's concept of reality: "Thus one species of evil is balanced by another; thus the fury of one element is repressed by the power of the other. In the midst of this great, this astonishing equipoise Man struggles and lives" (122). But this burst of light comes as the conclusion to a discussion of the control of rodents, and its radiance immediately flickers out, quenched in the renewed flow of practical information. The farmer of this sketch is a James *manqué*, a characterization that falters between the plowman of reality and the farmer of feelings. The four little letters that he writes would seem to represent a crucial step in the process by which Crèvecoeur approached the final conception embodied in the *Letters*, for in them he discovered the rudiments of the fictional framework and the outlines of the central consciousness that he was later to employ. At this stage, the meaning of the American experience still eluded him, and in its place he constructed an informal treatise on American husbandry, as if he were hesitant to venture beyond the routines and the artifacts of his own daily life.

Chapter V, "Liberty of Worship," and Chapter VI, "The English and the French before the Revolution," exhibit no such fear of generalization. Like Chapter III, which it seems designed to precede, "Liberty of Worship" attempts to describe and analyze American society at large by the method of the case history. Its central idea, that the chief blessing of religious pluralism is its capacity to absorb and neutralize rabid sectarianism, shows the influence of Raynal's anti-clericalism; but the tone and strategy of the essay are clearly those of Crèvecoeur's own American farmer. Although no epistolary elements are present, the speaker reveals his identity by his constant appeal to his familiar knowledge of the religious habits of the farming communities close to the frontier. Like James in "What Is an American" and like the unnamed persona of "Reflections on the Manners of the Americans," he relies heavily on the case history, here the unfortunate career of a neighboring farmer who was bitten by the bug of theological controversy. In general, the essay is a detailed development of the viewpoints and examples which appear in the three pages that "What Is an American" devotes to the subject of religion in America, but, like "Reflections on the Manners of the American," its rather sour sampling of experience in America runs counter to the buoyant mood of the first few *Letters*.

"The English and the French before the Revolution," on the other hand, bears no relation whatsoever to the materials of the *Letters*. For the most part, it is a nostalgic reminiscence of the simple and happy life led by the French in Canada before the British conquest, one of the rare occasions on which Crèvecoeur confronts the reader without a mask before his face. Developing, as it does, the contrast between the tranquil French and the quarrelsome English, the essay works to undermine two of the key doctrines of the *Letters;* for the French achieved their happiness in spite of a monolithic and hierarchical religious structure and an arbitrary and incompetent government. But in this little sketch, written about 1776, the chief sources of evil are the Anglo-Saxon race and the spirit of rebellion, both of which are represented in the person of George Washington, the murderer of Captain Jumonville in 1754 and now, by a monstrous irony, the idol of a misguided France. Slight though it is, the sketch supplies the earliest indication in Crèvecoeur's English manuscripts of his bitter response to the Revolution, a response which dominates the six remaining chapters of the *Sketches*.

In these last chapters, the voice and perspective are those of the farmer, but his subjects are no longer the techniques and problems of colonial agriculture or the influence of the American environment on social attitudes and behavior; his single theme is the destructiveness of war. He is no longer the plowman or the student of settlement but the melancholy annalist of the tragedies that the war brings to the lives of private citizens:

> Journals, memoirs, elaborate essays shall not fail hereafter to commemorate the heroes who have made their appearance on this new American stage, to the end that Europe may either lavishly praise or severely censure their virtues and their faults. It requires the inquisitive eye of an unnoticed individual mixing in crowds to find out and select for private amusement more obscure, though not less pathetic scenes. Scenes of sorrow and affliction are equally moving to the bowels of humanity. Find them where you will, there is a strange but peculiar sort of pleasure in contemplating them; it is a mournful feast for some particular souls. (228)

As the witnessing man in the crowd, his view is at close range, specific and immediate: "it is the individual object as it lies lowly prostrate which I wish to describe. I can encompass it; I can view it in all situations; and the limited impressions admit within my mind a possibility of retracing them" (229). The curious emotional detachment implied here is maintained throughout these chapters. Their background is the same as that of James's final letter—the disintegration of the social and moral order amid the chaos and violence of internecine warfare—but they have little of the impassioned personal involvement that dominates Letter XII. Now the farmer is truly the man in the crowd, the onlooker and recorder, rather than the actor and sufferer.

The objects which his restricted view encompasses comprise a gallery of victims, and their histories comprise an anthology of tales of blighted hope and unmerited misery. Chapter VII, "The Man of Sorows," recalls the scene of the caged Negro in the *Letters*; for it is centered on a tableau of excruciating physical torment: the agony of a suspected Tory collaborator who is tortured and hanged by a party of Patriot militia before the eyes of his wife and children. But, unlike the scene in Letter IX, this sketch has no symbolic overtones. The atrocity is not the vehicle of metaphysical statement but is offered simply as documentary evidence of the collapse of a society, an instance of the "rage of civil discord" that follows the breakdown of the machinery of legal and social subordination.

Nevertheless, the scene, as well as others like it, is not without its effect on the annalist who records it; for, since the society which is tumbling around him is his own, he shares in the shock of James's disillusionment: "Could I have ever thought that a people of cultivators, who knew nothing but their ploughs and the management of their rural economies, should be found to possess, like the more ancient nations of Europe, the embryos of these propensities which now stain our society?" (178). Here, as at the conclusion of the *Letters*, the Old World has overtaken the New. The dream of an American Eden is tenable no longer, for "Men are the same in all ages and in all countries"; everywhere a "strange fatality . . . seems to preside over all the actions of men" (179, 181). The representative American is now not the fortunate Andrew but men like this victim of the Patriot inquisition; for "Human society presents here nothing but tears and groans, and every species of calamity" (181–82).

The cheerful lineaments of Andrew are still harder to find in Chapter IX where, effacing himself altogether, the farmer presents the "History of Mrs. B. An Epitome of All the Misfortunes Which Can Possibly Overtake a New Settler, as Related by Herself." The daughter of a minister in an established community in the East, Mrs. B. is plunged into an unfamiliar world of hardship and danger when her husband decides to try his hand at farming on the frontier. Cheated by land agents, subjected to arduous journeys through the wilderness, desolated by marauders in a dispute between rival land companies, Mrs. B. and her husband at length achieve a measure of tranquillity and prosperity on a homestead near the banks of the Susquehanna.

With the coming of the Revolution, however, her trials resume: "What we had hitherto suffered was a sting of bees; we have received the wounds since which came from much more malevolent beings" (212). As suspected Tories, they undergo a variety of petty persecutions; still worse, her two oldest sons join the party of the persecutors by enlisting in the Patriot militia. A third son is captured by Indians and taken to Canada. At last the harassments by the Patriots force Mrs. B. and her husband to abandon their farm and move to the nearby settlement of Wyoming, which they reach just before it is devastated by a band of Tories and Indians. In the battle, Mrs. B.'s son-in-law is killed, and she and the rest of her family determine to flee the frontier. In the course of their retreat, however, her husband, one of her sons, and her infant grandchild successively fall victim to the smallpox and die. Mrs. B. lives on, nearly blind and penniless: "Such has been the singular fate, the long peregrination, the total ruin of a family once possessed of three good estates, born and bred of decent parents, endowed with good education; now half destroyed and now reduced to own not a single foot of land" (219-20).

The male counterpart of Mrs. B. is S. K., "The American Belisarius" of Chapter XI. According to the narrator, S. K. had founded a flourishing settlement in the wilderness; and there he had made a career of good works, liberally sharing his bounty and his advice with his less fortunate neighbors. But the outbreak of the Revolution gives those who envy his prosperity and reputation the chance to work the downfall of "this princely farmer" (233). He is accused of sympathizing with the British cause, his property is confiscated, and he is driven into the woods to be hunted by the militia and their dogs. Although the narrator is outraged by the persecution of his friend, S. K. bears it all with Christlike mildness; indeed, upon learning that one of the pursuing militiamen has received no pay for his duty, S. K. offers him two wagonloads of hay as compensation. When he is at last captured and tried, S. K. is, to the surprise of all, released on bail: "Like Belisarius of old, he is returned to live in that small part of his own house which is allotted him for his habitation; there to behold once more the extensive havoc which surrounds him; and to contemplate in gloomy despair the overthrow of his wife's reason and the reunion of all the physical evil that could possibly befall him, without resources and without hope" (245).

In all three of these exemplary tales, the curve of experience thus parallels the trajectory of James's fall from happiness in the *Letters*. But none of them has the power of the story of James, for they lack adequate development and psychological credibility. The tortured householder of Chapter VI comes before us without a history and devoid of characterization; he is the victim incarnate, a figure from a propaganda poster. Still less moving are the histories of Mrs. B. and S. K. Like the misfortunes of the old woman in *Candide*, the recurrent disasters that plague the career of Mrs. B. gather a comic effect; for, in a world in which everything goes wrong, each successive catastrophe diminishes in its capacity to compel pity and becomes, instead, the mechanical repetition of farce. Nearly as long-suffering as Mrs. B., the American Belisarius staggers under the additional handicap of his impossible virtue. Crèvecoeur's art is insufficient to sustain his comparison of S. K.'s tribulations to "the suffering of Thy Son, the Moral Legislator, the Pattern of Mankind" (238). Annoyed by the moral arrogance which S. K. parades before his benighted neighbors, the irreverent reader may too easily find himself cheering on the persecutors.

The three remaining Revolutionary sketches are, in their various ways, more successful than their predecessors. Chapter VII, "The Wyoming Massacre," constitutes the single attempt at broad historical narration in the English manuscripts. The sweeping, generalized point of view in this account of the infamous attack of July 3, 1778, by Butler's Indians and Tories upon the settlements in northeastern Pennsylvania is managed with considerable skill. The balanced portrayal of the fears and animosities that actuated both the settlers and the Indians in their dealings prior to the massacre produces a poignant sense of inevitability. The complex details of the action are rendered with perfect clarity, the emphases are appropriate, and the narration as a whole is given the shaped completeness that distinguishes the best of the anecdotes in the *Letters*. Indeed, in the vivid handling of the crowd scenes, in the focus on human combat against the background of the tremendous wilderness, and in the dramatic contrast between the ragged retreat of the survivors and the hopeful mood of their first approach to Wyoming, one is reminded of the masterly effects of the narratives of Cooper and Parkman.

Chapter X, "The Frontier Woman," returns to the view at close range of an individual participant in the turmoil of civil war; but the subject is the persecutor rather than his victim. In this brief, overwritten, but nevertheless powerful sketch, a remorseful Tory terrorist tells his story to the farmer. Looking back upon his career of slaughter, he wonders at his own indifference to the horror of his acts, at the capacity of man to take "a singular pleasure" in shedding the blood of his fellow man. From his retrospection he can salvage only one consolation. Once, as a member of a raiding party of Tories and Indians, he entered the farmhouse that he was assigned to destroy and was confronted by a young mother who, setting aside the two babies she was nursing, bared her breast to his tomahawk. Restrained by a sudden impulse, he withheld his blow and persuaded his companions to leave her unharmed. Although the Tory is addicted to sentimental exclamation more appropriate to the stage than to the frontier—"Live, honest woman, live!" he tells the frightened mother (224)—the sketch succeeds as a study of the anesthetized sensibility of the terrorist and of the torment of guilt which follows the return of feeling. On its tiny scale, the sketch represents one of Crèvecoeur's most penetrating explorations of the psychology of violence.

The analysis of evil continues in "Landscapes," the final chapter of the *Sketches*, but in vastly different terms. This piece, the most interesting of Crèvecoeur's wartime writings, is cast in the form of drama. Although portions of Letters I and XI faintly suggest the dramatic mode in their heavy reliance on dialogue, "Landscapes," by contrast, is a full-fledged play of some eighty pages, equipped with the apparatus of stage directions and divided into six major scenes. And the stress is less upon the violence and pathos of the war than upon the greed and corruption that it fosters. The subject is the activities of half a day in the life of Deacon Beatus, chairman of a provincial Committee of Public Safety, colonel in the Patriot militia, and commissioner for selling Tory estates; the object is the exposure of the "hypocrisy, slyness, cupidity, inhumanity and abuse of power in these petty country despots" (254).

The six scenes, or "landscapes" as Crèvecoeur calls them, allow one to witness the Deacon at ease in the nest of vipers that is his family, threatening a wealthy Tory with imprisonment and the confiscation of his property, bullying the owner of the local tavern into the offer of free refreshment, terrorizing and robbing the wife of a Tory squire whom he has driven into hiding, and coldly rebuking the rage and despair of a woman whose husband he has had hanged. In addition to the Deacon, his family, and his victims, the characters of the play include two *raisonneurs*— a traveling American gentleman and his Russian companion—and a gallery of agents of the Patriot oppression: the militiamen Lieutenant Splash, Colonel Templeman, Captain Shoreditch, and Major Popino, and the newmade rebel squire Aaron Blue-Skin. The result is a detailed and bitterly satiric vignette of a Yankee reign of terror, in every way the most credible and telling of Crèvecoeur's studies of the poisonous effects of the war.

Like the rest of the contents of the *Sketches*, "Landscapes," effective though it is, was wisely omitted from the published *Letters*; for the detachment of its savage irony is utterly inappropriate to James in any of his several phases. Moreover, it is difficult to see how "Landscapes" could be arranged in any conceivable combination with the other sketches to form a volume which would approach the *Letters* in unity and coherence. Like "Thoughts of an American Farmer on Various Rural Subjects," "Landscapes" is an entity in itself; and there are indications that Crèvecoeur at one time considered publishing it separately. Although the little essay which introduces the play carries on the epistolary pretense, it is designed to stand by itself and makes no reference to any preceding letter. And to the manuscript of "Landscapes," Crèvecoeur appended a list of designs for four copperplate illustrations, clear evidence of an intention to publish. Whatever plans Crèvecoeur may have had for the ultimate disposition of "Landscapes" were, however, never realized; and it appears in the *Sketches* as one more fragment in a gathering of fragments.

II *Thought and Attitude in the* Sketches

Upon its first publication in 1925, *Sketches of Eighteenth Century America* seemed to require a general revaluation of Crèvecoeur's intellectual position. Accustomed by the traditional reading of the *Letters* to regard its author as a Rousseauistic celebrator of sentiment and nature, as a tenderhearted and softheaded idealist, and as a panegyrist of all things American, students of Crèvecoeur were startled and delighted by what seemed to be a totally new note in the *Sketches*, a strong and often pessimistic strain of critical realism. This was the light in which the editors of the *Sketches* presented their collection to the public in their accompanying announcements in various periodicals and in the elaborate introductory essays which they included in the volume.[3] Surprised by the extraordinary "realism" of Crèvecoeur's treatment of rural life and finding in the newly published Loyalist sketches "not only the most effective and imaginative work in either of Crèvecoeur's English books, but also the most effective work of the imagination that we possess in America by an American during that century," John Brooks Moore proposed "The Rehabilitation of Crèvecoeur."[4] Howard Rice was soon to suggest, however, that the political focus of many of the sketches and the sardonic view of American experience which they express represent only a passing phase in the development of Crèvecoeur's attitudes, his immediate response to the Revolution, and therefore reveal no essentially new element in his thought.[5]

Surely the directness and bitterness with which the *Sketches* condemns the spread of violence and the overthrow of established order in Revolutionary America are unprecedented in Crèvecoeur's other published writings; but, as a whole, the work develops no ideas and attitudes that violate the broad system of meanings in the *Letters*, no clue to a "secret" body of opinions which the other writings carefully conceal. The doctrine that in agriculture reside man's most natural occupation and the surest source of personal happiness and social order is just as central to the *Sketches* as it is to the *Letters*. Thus throughout the long complaint of Chapter III, the delights of ownership, of close contact with nature, of country social festivities, and of rural domesticity keep breaking in. What is new in the portrayal of the farmer's life in the *Sketches* are not the fundamental attitudes but the wealth of factual information—the effects of the clearing of forests and swamps on the water table, the problems of rural indebtedness, the use of frozen rivers as avenues to markets—that makes the book an invaluable, though largely neglected, source for historians of colonial agriculture.

Similarly, in those chapters upon which the Revolution does not intrude, the *Sketches* traces an image of America at large that follows the concepts of Raynal as faithfully as does the *Letters*. The New World is still pictured as the "country of hospitality and plenty," where farmers go "not to that bed of slavery or sorrow as is the case in Europe with people of their class, but on the substantial collection of honest feathers picked and provided by the industrious wife" (45, 46). America remains the asylum for the wretched of Europe, who are invited to "avoid the fetters of their country, and come in shoals to partake of our toils as well as of our happiness" (48). As in the *Letters,* the foundation of the prosperity and happiness of the colonies is the simplicity and variety of their religious practices, the system of freeholds, and the mild exercise of governmental authority. The basic conception of America in the first five chapters of the *Sketches* is identical to that which underlies the rosy first half of the *Letters*: it is the place where human nature, unrestrained and unperverted, can renew itself and regain its pristine vigor.

But, in the opening chapters of the *Sketches,* the doubts and misgivings about the quality of raw human nature that are present only in the undercurrent of the first half of the *Letters* receive direct and emphatic expression. To the farmer of Chapter IV, man is the supreme predator, "a huge monster who devours everything and will suffer nothing to live in peace in his neighbourhood," "a selfish being" (117, 145). The settlers of Chapter III, released from the restraints of law, religion, and the conventions of an established society, become new men, to be sure, but the failings of human nature, as well as its virtues, are given free rein: "If it is not 'bellum ominum contra omnes,' 'tis a general mass of keenness and sagacious [sagacity?] acting against another mass of equal sagacity; 'tis caution against caution. Happy, when it does not degenerate into fraud against fraud" (78). Similarly, external nature is a mixed blessing; for, if "bountiful Nature is kind to us on the one hand, on the other she wills that we shall purchase her kindness not only with sweats and labour but with vigilance and care" (121). The striking element of the first group of sketches is the balance that the very syntax of passages like this one conveys, a poise between the light of a Letter II and the darkness of a Letter IX.

That balance is lost in the plunge toward melancholy and outrage in the Revolutionary sketches. But, once again, the difference between the thought of these sketches and that of the *Letters* seems primarily a matter of focus and emphasis. Working without knowledge of the manuscripts from which the *Sketches* was later assembled, Julia Mitchell was nevertheless able to identify accurately Crèvecoeur's basic stance in the conflict—that of a neutral appalled by the violence and compassionate for the suffering of both sides.[6] Indeed, the Revolutionary sketches reiterate the attitudes that are explicitly stated in "Distresses of a Frontier-Man" in the *Letters*: loyalty to the government of Britain, qualified by a sense of abandonment and betrayal as its agents turn their attacks upon innocent colonists; abhorrence at the idea of rebellion and the disruption of the social order, qualified by a sympathy for the interests of one's friends and neighbors. Thus the sketches can depict the agony of the Man of Sorrows, the victim of the Patriot inquisition, and the devastation of Wyoming, the victim of the Tory raiders; they can probe the motives of the Loyalist guerrilla and of the rebel committee chairman. The true enemy is neither one side or the other but the war itself.

The subject of these sketches is the transformation that has been worked by the symbolic snake of the *Letters*, that hideous metamorphosis by which plowmen become slaughterers and deacons become petty tyrants. Truly, "Men in a state of civil war are no longer the same"; for the controversy has "disseminated among them the most horrid poison" (180, 192), enflaming their enmities and paralyzing their industry. The Revolution, in every sense, represents the triumph of evil. Its ideals are spurious, the concoctions of a few self-seeking deceivers: "Ambition . . . an exorbitant love of power and thirst of riches, a certain impatience of government, by some people called liberty,—all these motives, clad under the garb of patriotism and even of constitutional reason, have been the secret but true foundation of this, as well as of many other revolutions" (251).

Once set in motion, the war releases all the latent viciousness that the social order had hitherto held in check, bringing to the top those who "were, before these times, mostly poor, obscure, and unnoticed; great psalm-singers, zealous religionists who would not have cracked a nut on the Sabbath,—no, not for any worldly consideration" (247). Now these "men of plausible countenances, sleek-haired, but possessed at the same time of great duplicity of heart" (248), give vent to their hidden malice and avarice, at home in the envenomed world of war. The viewpoint is that of the established New York landholders and merchants with whom Crèvecoeur associated during his residence at Pine

Hill, men who regarded with distaste the ultra-pious and ultra-political Yankees who had settled in rural New York in the first phase of their migration westward and who now took the lead in the cause of rebellion.

But this attitude is also sanctioned by Raynal, who looked with displeasure upon the movement for independence and whose *Histoire philosophique* was reissued by Rivington's Tory press during the British occupation of New York City. More important, it was the inevitable viewpoint of a man possessed of a constitutional aversion to violence and turmoil, whose political philosophy advocated the relaxation of restraint, and whose deepest fears centered on the innate savagery that the removal of restraint might release. What is missing from the *Sketches* is the full descent from the enjoyment of that philosophy to the realization of those fears, as it is described by the experience of James. For none of the many masks of the *Sketches* confronts the world with quite the confident innocence with which the Farmer of the *Letters* begins his correspondence.

III *The Art of the* Sketches

If the thought of the *Sketches* bears a close relationship to that of the *Letters*, the modes and techniques of several of the individual selections embody significant departures from the practice of the *Letters* and thereby offer additional evidence of the range and versatility of Crèvecoeur's art. It should be emphasized, however, that all of the sketches are early drafts, not yet subjected to the revision that would surely have preceded publication, and hence are marked not only by the stylistic eccentricities which the editors struggled to regularize but often by drastic lapses in coherence, by repetitions, and, most important, by inadequate development of the full significance of the material. Thus, by comparison with the *Letters*, the sketches are notably deficient in symbolic resonance.

As a group, of course, they lack the sustained context that permits the images of the *Letters* to function as motifs, accumulating and subtly varying meaning with each appearance. But more than that, the imagery within the individual sketches too often remains inert descriptive fact, its symbolic possibilities unrealized. The farmer of Chapter IV tells of finding in his woods a flowering vine intertwined with the branches of a sassafras tree. Struck by their beauty, he moved the two plants to his garden and presented them as a gift to his daughter. The same incident appears in the French *Lettres* of 1784, where it becomes the basis of an elaborate emblematic treatment of the love between father and daughter, typified by the supporting tree and the dependent vine. But here the two plants are offered simply as a botanical curiosity and serve to introduce a discussion of the economic benefits that would accrue to the colonists if they would drink a brew made from the native sassafras instead of enriching the London merchants by importing tea from India.

Or again, in this same chapter, the kingbird and the bees of Letter II make an appearance. But where James's kingbird had functioned as the symbol of the abuse of power and the bees which he liberates from its craw had enacted an allegory of the American rebirth of the victim of European tyranny, the farmer of Chapter IV remains on the literal level, sorry that he occasionally must shoot the beautiful and otherwise useful kingbird because of its regrettable habit of feeding on bees. In both instances, the sketch seems to embody Crèvecoeur's first conception, the raw material of art rather than its end result.

For all their lack of finish, however, the sketches offer several well-constructed examples of the mode which apparently came most easily to Crèvecoeur—the straightforward narrative. As has been seen, many of these narratives are offered as case histories, as representative illustrations of the tendencies of American experience. In a few of the sketches, however, narratives appear which serve no expository purpose but which, like the anecdote of Andrew's encounter with the Indians, are offered for their intrinsic interest. There are even a few rudimentary tall tales, like the one that Crèvecoeur appropriated from Captain Carver's account of his improbable adventures:

> In the summer our meadows and fields are beautifully illuminated by an immense number of fire-flies, which in the calm of the evening sweetly wander here and there at a small distance from the ground. By their alternate glows of light they disseminate a kind of universal splendour, which, being always contrasted with the darkness of the night, has a most surprising effect. I have often

read by their assistance; that is I have taken one carefully by the wings and, carrying it along the lines of my book, I have, when thus assisted by these living flambeaux, perused whole pages, and then thankfully dismissed these little insect-stars. (p. 128)[7]

The mood and materials of this little anecdote are precisely those of Letter II. In a world of poetic plowmen and insectile illumination, the reader is not permitted to raise the questions that entomology and opthalmology may suggest. In the same sketch, the farmer again suspends his discussion of colonial agriculture long enough to tell a very different kind of tale: the sentimental story of the rescue of a lost white child by the Indian Tewenissa and his sagacious dog. The ostensible justification of the anecdote is its service as illustration of a few brief remarks on the breed of American dogs; but, since the illustration is seven or eight times longer than the discussion it is meant to support, the reader suspects that it is there for other reasons, one of which, surely, is its vivid emotional coloring. The pathetic distress of the family of the missing child, the tender concern of the Indian, the joy of the parents when the child is recovered, and the noble magnanimity of Tewenissa's response to the settlers' gratitude are all rendered with a careful eye to their appeal to the feelings. Like the banquet which is held in celebration of the rescue, the anecdote provides "a feast for the soul" (134). If the diet of sentiment is apt to cloy, the story is nevertheless a remarkably early American example of the tale of tears and smiles that Irving later popularized in his *Sketch Book*.

The *Letters*, of course, furnishes ample evidence of Crèvecoeur's narrative skill; but it offers no real precedent for his experiment with the drama in "Landscapes." In view of the state of American drama in 1777, the probable date of the manuscript, it is hard to overstate the extent of Crèvecoeur's achievement. With the exception of a few feeble political farces and satires like Mercy Warren's Revolutionary War plays, the dramatic uses of the American scene were virtually unexplored. The playwright generally credited with the first exploitation of American characters and manners, Royall Tyler, was not to produce *The Contrast* until 1787. If "Landscapes" is surely not immensely superior to *The Contrast*, as one critic has maintained,[8] it does compare favorably with Tyler's play.

Although "Landscapes" lacks the tightness of Tyler's structure and his rather sophisticated awareness of stage effects, it embodies a far bolder and more original concept than does *The Contrast*. Tyler patterned the structure and materials of his play closely on the model of British sentimental comedy, but Crèvecoeur appears to have worked without benefit of any prior example. His play is an eighteenth-century attempt at a slice of life, a careful investigation into the sordid daily routine of a village tyrant. His object is to render the true image of the new America, not the soaring eagle, "the august bird arrayed with majestic feathers; 'tis only the nest in which it was hatched, composed of sticks and twigs cemented with dirt, lined with clay, whence has sprung this new master of the sky" (250). No comedy beyond the grim ironies of hypocrisy, no love plot, and no happy ending serve to lighten the relentless satiric realism.

"Landscapes" is scarcely a well-made play. The pace is slow and the action repetitious. The structure of both the individual scenes and the play as a whole tends to be anticlimactic. The dialogue of the sympathetic characters is stilted and too frequently serves to provide the author with an occasion for speechifying. But, pompous though virtue may be in Crèvecoeur's play, it never attains the absolute rigidity and artificiality under which Tyler's Colonel Manly staggers, nor are the manners and attitudes of the low-life characters reduced by caricature to the comic idiocy of Tyler's Jonathan. If Tyler is to be credited with inventing the stage Yankee, Crèvecoeur must be acknowledged as the first writer to explore the serious implications of the Yankee spirit.

That spirit which Irving was to touch upon and which Cooper was to probe in depth is here laid bare in the characterizations of Deacon Beatus and Aaron Blue-Skin. Restless, versatile, acquisitive, and shrewd, they quote the Bible and cheat their neighbors with equal ease. Like Cooper's Steadfast Dodge and Aristabulus Bragg, they are at once the manipulators of popular opinion and the creatures of it. "What will the people, the neighbours think?" (267) is always the Deacon's first consideration. From the analysis of these "veteran Puritans" arises the central theme of the play, a theme which, in its seriousness and abiding relevance, makes the ideas of *The Contrast* seem strained and inconsequential. That American simplicity might be corrupted by the importation of English manners, Tyler's announced concern, must have seemed, even in 1787, a pretense, a strategem to permit the piquant juxtaposition of contrasting manners on which the play is constructed.

But Crèvecoeur's embittered survey of a society in which religion masks the worship of wealth and influence, in which law becomes the expression of public hysteria, in which government functions as an instrument of exploitation, and in which culture becomes the object of an envious contempt raises issues that have persisted with a disturbing tenacity throughout the course of the American experience. For all its technical clumsiness, "Landscapes" would seem to merit an important place in the history of American drama, co-equal, at least, with *The Contrast* as a pioneering use of American materials. Still more surely, it deserves recognition as an early and penetrating example of social criticism in American literature, one that makes the satires of a Trumbull or a Hopkinson seem pallid and contrived.

"Landscapes" represents the most radical departure from the various modes of the *Letters*, but the diverse contents of the *Sketches* supply still other indications of Crèvecoeur's interest in experimentation with form and technique. One of the most interesting is provided by the sketch which serves as the opening chapter of the gathering, "A Snow-Storm as It Affects the American Farmer." Far more than "On the Situation, Feelings, and Pleasures of an American Farmer," its closest parallel in the *Letters*, "A Snow-Storm" is an attempt to render in prose the substance, themes, and effects of the Thomsonian descriptive poem. Stimulated by the enormous popularity of James Thomson's *The Seasons* (1726-30) and heavily influenced by John Dyer's rural poetry, the descriptive poem—a lengthy compendium of landscape depiction, moral and philosophical rumination, narrative episodes, and agricultural advice—became a major mode of eighteenth-century verse both in England and on the Continent. In its treatment of rural life, the descriptive poem is closer to the manner of the *Georgics* than of the *Eclogues*, more realistic and practical than stylized and idyllic. Its approach to nature is full of curiosity and admiration, tending at once toward Deistic speculation and Romantic awe. Its structure is often keyed to the passage of a unit of time—a day, a season, a year—and the changes in nature and in human activities which occur within that span of time.

Marked by all these characteristics and among the most carefully shaped of all of Crèvecoeur's writings, "A Snow-Storm" is, in a very meaningful sense, a prose-poem, an American georgic. The opening sentences of the sketch firmly establish the perspective of contemplative wonder by postulating that no man "of the least degree of sensibility" can survey the natural world around him "without involuntarily being struck either with awe or admiration in beholding some of the elementary conflicts in the midst of which he lives" (39). The subject of the sketch is to be the "rigour" and the "vehemence" of winter in the Northern colonies and the focus is to be on the response of the farmer to the season, "that energetic circle of foresight, knowledge, and activity which fill the space of five months" (40).

The main development of the sketch begins as Crèvecoeur's farmer makes his preparations for the coming cold, supplying by his good example a multitude of agricultural precepts and exhibiting the dignity and importance of his way of life. The field of vision takes in the ominous changes in the weather: the great fall rains, the first severe frost, the "short interval of smoke and mildness, called the Indian Summer" (41); and then, in a passage that precisely parallels the substance and movement of Thomsonian descriptive verse, the onslaught of a winter storm:

> The wind . . . shifts to the northeast; the air becomes bleak and then intensely cold; the light of the sun becomes dimmed as if an eclipse had happened; a general night seems coming on. At last, imperceptible atoms make their appearance; they are few and descend slowly, a sure prognostic of a great snow. Little or no wind is as yet felt. By degrees the number as well as the size of these white particles is increased; they descend in larger flakes; a distant wind is heard; the noise swells and seems to advance; the new element at last appears and overspreads everything. In a little time the heavy clouds seem to approach nearer the earth and discharge a winged flood, driving along towards the southwest, howling at every door, roaring in every chimney, whistling with asperous sound through the naked limbs of the trees. . . .
> (41–42)

With the advent of the blizzard, a "general alarm is spread

through the farm" (42); the animals are led to their stables; and Tom, the Negro slave, is dispatched on horseback to retrieve the children from school. This last detail becomes the occasion for an extended narrative episode, for Rachel, the daughter of a poor widow is among the snowbound children. But, unlike the peasant who is lost in a sea of snow in Thomson's *Winter,* little Rachel is rescued by honest Tom and returned to her tearful mother. After a succession of vignettes of winter life on the farm—the tasks and recreations of the season of snow—the sketch reaches its ending: "A long ramble like this through a cold Canadian storm requires rest, silence, and sleep. After so long an excursion we may with propriety wish each other good night" (50).

There are georgic strains in the other sketches, notably in the series of correspondences that are drawn between the republic of insects and the republic of men in "Ant-Hill Town" and in the horticultural didacticism of "Thoughts of an American Farmer on Various Rural Subjects"; but "A Snow-Storm" is unique in its thoroughgoing observance of the conventions of eighteenth-century georgic poetry. Nearly all the elements that serve to define the type are present: the delight in the grand and stormy aspects of nature, the presentation of useful knowledge, the celebration of the life of the husbandman, the interest in landscape, the employment of narrative episodes and genre scenes, the attention to the behavior of animals, and the overriding concern with the interrelation of man and nature. The triumph of the sketch is the ease and naturalness with which it adapts the conventions of descriptive verse to the uses of prose and to the depiction of what is always presented as a distinctively American setting and way of life. Altogether, it is Crèvecoeur's most engaging piece of writing.

Not only does "A Snow-Storm" begin the *Sketches* on a georgic note, but it establishes connections with an art form still farther removed from the ordinary province of prose—painting. In this sketch, the analogies between Crèvecoeur's scenic techniques and the methods of painting are one more reminder of the closeness of the sketch to the concerns and devices of descriptive poetry; for descriptive verse had long been regarded, and sometimes condemned, as an attempt to fuse literature and the visual arts. The scenes of the snow-covered trees and cattle and the vignettes of the family around the hearth in "A Snow-Storm" are thus components of the general literary tradition which Crèvecoeur was following; but, as Stanley T. Williams has observed, a certain pictorial quality is present throughout the *Sketches*, a tendency to portray figures and actions "as if arrested in painting or sculpture."[9] Thus in "The Wyoming Massacre," the narrative pauses and fixes upon a specific image amid the settlers' retreat from the devastated village:

> Here you might see a poor starved horse as weak and emaciated as themselves, given them perhaps by the enemy as a last boon. The poor beast was loaded with a scanty feather-bed serving as a saddle which was fastened on him with withes and bark. On it sat a wretched mother with a child at her breast, another on her lap, and two more placed behind her, all broiling in the sun, accompanied in this pilgrimage of tribulation by the rest of the family creeping slowly along, leading at a great distance behind a heifer once wild and frolicsome but now tamed by want and hunger; a cow, perhaps, with hollow flanks and projecting ribs closed the train. . . . (205–6)

The painterly quality of the description is exhibited in the concern for composition that places the gaunt horse and its burden in the central foreground and leads into the background by picking out the remaining members of the procession, and in the bold emphasis of details—the makeshift saddle and the bony bodies of the animals—that establish the primary meanings of the scene.

This habit of adopting the artist's detached point of view, of gazing upon scenes of agony and misery with a painter's eye for composition, becomes a standard device in the Revolutionary War sketches, a major means of attaining the ironic compound of horror and objectivity that is absolutely foreign to the *Letters*. The most striking example of the technique is furnished by "The Man of Sorrows," in which everything seems designed to build toward the dramatic tableau that concludes the sketch:

> What a subject for a painter who delights to represent mournful events! What a field for a judge and master of the passions! A man leaning against a tree, hardly recovered from the agonies of death, still visible in the livid hue and altered lineaments of his

face, still weak and trembling, his mind agitated with the most tumultuous thoughts, wracked by the most anxious suspense, hearing his third and final doom. At a little distance his wife, sitting on a log, almost deprived of her reason. At a more considerable distance, his house, with all his children crowded at the door, restrained by amazement and fear from following their mother, each exhibiting strong expressions of curiosity and terror, agreeable to their different ages. I can conceive the peculiar nature of all these colourings, but where would the painter find the originals of these faces[?] [W]ho, unmoved, could behold the different scenes of this awful drama? (191)

Crèvecoeur's attempts to make language do the work of the visual arts may remind the reader of the picturesque effects of Irving and Cooper, but here the attempt is not only to enlarge the resources of literature by drawing on those of a sister art but, in the best of these passages, to manipulate auctorial distance. The analogy to the subject of a painting is drawn and then denied. In the scene of turmoil, there is no place for the serene artist, palette in hand; in the scene of anguish, there is no possibility for the painter's dispassionate poise. The detachment of these sketches is at last only a gesture, a momentary stepping back by which the witness seeks to retain control of his emotions in the face of the compelling horror before him.

Perhaps, then, the chief intrinsic value of *Sketches of Eighteenth Century America* resides in the bold and rewarding excursions that Crèvecoeur conducts into the fields of the drama, the descriptive poem, and painting—areas that the *Letters* left unexplored. Indeed, to the reader concerned with Crèvecoeur's artistic method and its development, even the failures and false starts that are preserved in the *Sketches* are of interest; for they give insight into the workshop in which the *Letters* was fashioned. They suggest that the perspective of the American Farmer was not easily come by, that it was achieved only after a number of attempts to identify and define the role and to find the voice. To the reader interested in Crèvecoeur the man, the *Sketches* is more revealing than the *Letters;* for the raw manuscripts from which the book was assembled constitute, in effect, a writer's journal. One feels that its materials are far closer to Crèvecoeur's own direct experience than are those of any of his other published writings. But the last impression left by the *Sketches* is regret, regret that the manifest promise contained in these manuscripts was never to be fulfilled, that a writer who displayed every symptom of artistic growth and who responded to America with the most intense love and the most intense hatred should be diverted from his path, be required to adopt a different tongue, and be frozen in the attitudes of a public official, no longer an inhabitant of the land that nourished his art, but an emissary to it.

CHAPTER *5*

The French Writings

I *America Revised*

IN THE SUMMER of 1782, a year after his return to France, Crèvecoeur undertook the preparation of a French version of the *Letters*. The English volume, published six months before, had attracted considerable attention; and Madame d'Houdetot and her literary friends gave their flattering encouragement to the project. Delayed by the disappearance of the manuscript during the writing of the book and by difficulties in securing a license from the government for its publication, the two volumes of *Lettres d'un Cultivateur Américain* at last appeared in December, 1784. The success of the *Lettres* was immediate and inevitable, for the book was accurately tailored to the interests and preconceptions of its French audience.

In the words of Lacretelle, who publicized and reviewed the new work in the influential *Mercure de France,* its author "is the Poet of America, as well as its Historian. His sensitive soul and his ardent imagination seize on every scene which strikes and moves him": the domestic bliss of the American farmer, the upward climb of the European immigrant, the humanitarianism of the Quakers, the hardships and heroism of the Revolution, the interesting ways of the Negro and the Indian. But most attractive of all is the figure of the author himself, "that man possessed of a character so simple, a spirit so energetic, a life so active," that man whose attempts to efface himself from his narratives fail to obscure his noble efforts on behalf of the oppressed and the suffering.[1]

If the points of Lacretelle's emphasis seem odd to the reader of the *Letters,* it is because the book which he describes is totally different in its design and its effects from its English predecessor.

It is true that Crèvecoeur made extensive use of the materials of the *Letters*. In one way or another, all but one of the English letters are represented in the *Lettres* of 1784, and that single exception, Letter X, was included in the third volume which Crèvecoeur added to the *Lettres* in the edition of 1787. But in their passage from the *Letters* to the *Lettres*, the contents of the English work were shifted in sequence and interspersed with new materials; most were subjected to a radical revision of form and substance. As a result, the design of the letters was shattered and their individual meanings drastically altered.

In the reworking of the English materials, James has vanished and with him have gone the unity which his sharply defined point of view provided and the poignant drama which his American experience enacted. In his place the reader is offered only "St. John," the compiler of the miscellaneous sketches, autobiographical narratives, newspaper clippings, and consular reports from which the *Lettres* is constructed—a figure who is eager to be identified with the goodhearted, inquisitive public official known as St. John de Crèvecoeur. The change is a saddening one; but, to make matters worse, some traces of the epistolary device linger on, in defiance of all logic and deprived of all function. The pretense, faintly maintained in the remnants from the *Letters* and all but abandoned in the other materials, is that the contents of the *Lettres* represent St. John's unlikely epistles to his correspondent "Wm. S——on Esq." between 1770 and 1786.

Indicative of the confused oscillation of the *Lettres* between fact and fiction, the name of the correspondent is a compliment to Crèvecoeur's New York friend William Seton, who is here forced to play the part of the traveling Englishman that James's Mr. F. B. had taken. "Voisin St. John," like James before him, has been persuaded by the reassurances of his minister to undertake the correspondence that his English friend requested, but this time no sharp-tongued wife takes part in the dialogue, for in the sentimentalized world of the *Lettres* there are no such creatures. And, like James, St. John has inherited a substantial farm in Carlisle, Pennsylvania, from his father. By the end of the first volume, however, the identity of the persona of the *Lettres* has become hopelessly confused. As St. John tells of his imprisonment in New York and of his voyage to Europe, he expresses his relief at finally reaching France, "my homeland, which I had not seen for twenty-seven years" (I, 461).

The integrity and clarity of the characterization of the persona, however, is much less important to the *Lettres* than to the *Letters*, because the function of that persona has changed. Only once, in the account of the visit to Bartram, does the *Letters* depart from the consciousness of James. Everything else comes through James, is colored by his response, and contributes to the evolution of his thoughts and feelings. But in the *Lettres*, St. John fills his correspondence with extracts from the letters of other private individuals, with samples of Indian oratory, and with reports of addresses to public assemblies; indeed, the invention of sources other than the central persona becomes one of the few imaginative elements in the book. Even some of the survivals from the *Letters* are subjected to the process. The second half of Letter XII, for example, in which James announces his desperate resolution to abandon white civilization and take up residence in a remote Indian village appears in the *Lettres* as a letter written by "Francis-H-Ur," an Irish settler at Cherry Valley in central New York. Increasingly, as the *Lettres* proceeds, the figure of the *Cultivateur Américain* dwindles; he is overshadowed by the autobiographical author and obscured among the ranks of competing personae.

If the shifts in sequence and in voice disrupt the pattern of significance which the *Letters* as a whole describes, drastic revisions of the contents produce equally profound changes in the meaning of the individual letters. The moderately Tory tone of the *Letters*, chiefly present in the first half of Letter XII, is replaced by a strident denouncement of British tyranny and by a wholehearted celebration of the Patriot cause. James, disgusted by the contradictory charges of the two sides, asks, "And after all, who will be the really guilty?" His answer is short and cynical: "Those most certainly who fail of success" (*Letters*, 279).

St. John of the *Lettres* poses the same question, but the route he takes is circuitous: "And after all, which party is the most guilty? the one which crosses the Ocean, in order to impose unjust taxes at the point of a bayonet, that which, on the pretext of duty, pillages and carries off everything it pleases, shoots, murders, burns, and converts a fertile country into a wasteland; or the one which, armed in its own defense, resists force with force

with a courage guided by humanity? Which one will be the most
guilty in the eyes of the tranquil spectator? The one which does
not suceed" (II, 262-63). In the passage from the *Lettres,* the
question is only rhetorical; and the response becomes merely a
display of worldly-wise irony, not a despairing rejection of all
political charges and appeals.

The adoption of a fervent anti-British bias is the most striking
new note in the *Lettres,* but it is, finally, a symptom of a far larger
and more significant change. For the view that now resolves political issues into clear-cut divisions between good and evil also
tends to organize the whole of reality into systems and schemes,
to simplify experience by forcing it into preconceived patterns.
In the *Letters,* doctrine and theory are in constant confrontation
with things as they are; and the resulting clash and tension are
among the most impressive features of the book. But in the *Lettres,* experience is no longer resilient and enigmatic in the face of
theory.

This larger change can be seen in a comparison of "On the
Situation, Feelings, and Pleasures, of an American Farmer" in the
Letters and its equivalent in the *Lettres,* "Pensées d'un cultivateur
américain, sur son sort & les plaisirs de la campagne," even though
the French version follows the English original more closely than
do most of the reworkings of the materials of the *Letters.* St. John,
it is clear, inhabits a far more orderly world than does James.
Whereas James's thoughts and impressions come crowding in as
they occur to him, the materials of the French letter are carefully
organized by topic and by their position in the seasonal cycle.
James's world is populated by contrarieties and contradictions: he
is struck by the harmonious and intricate workings of instinct,
and yet he does not hesitate to record the aggression of the wren
or the fury of the wasps. The epitome of his vision is the precarious relationship that he maintains with the hornets which catch
their prey on the very eyelids of his children.

But the natural world of St. John contains no looting wrens and
stinging insects. It must not, for they would violate the elaborate
set-piece which Crèvecoeur added to the English original–a
seven-page hymn to the soothing beauties of nature, in the course
of which St. John regrets that he cannot play the lyre, for he
longs "to sing of our American Naiads, our rural divinities, the

verdure of our mountains, the fertility of our valleys, the majesty of our rivers" (I, 80). This benign outlook enters into the smallest details of the French revision. Where, for example, James contemplates the miraculous transformation which the egg on his table might have undergone were it not for his gluttony, St. John concentrates on the miracle and omits all reference to his own frustration of it. If James's sketch of his daily life verges on the idyllic, St. John's is unabashedly a fantasy, a pretty pastoral that is tailored to conform precisely to the eighteenth-century literary image of country seclusion and innocence.

The process of radical simplification is applied with equal thoroughness to the materials which Crèvecoeur transferred to the *Lettres* from the English manuscripts that had not been published in the *Letters*. The reader of the *Sketches* is startled to find its rather harsh ingredients, nearly all of which are represented here in one way or another, softened and purified to the point of insipidity. "The American Belisarius" and "Landscapes" are excluded, too steeped in bitterness and Loyalism for salvage; but all the other Revolutionary War sketches are used. In every instance, the French version departs from its English predecessor in two ways: the burden of sentiment, already a substantial one, is increased; and the political attitudes are altered so as to throw sympathy on the rebels and to blacken the position of England.

Thus, in the transformation of "The Man of Sorrows" into the "Histoire de Joseph Wilson," Crèvecoeur adds comments on the extreme cruelty of the British raids along the frontier in an effort to justify the savagery of the Patriot militia in its inquisition of the suspected Tory collaborator. The effect is to shift the locus of evil from general human nature, with its addiction to violence, to a more comfortable source, perfidious Britain. In the blaze of the patriotic rhetoric that Crèvecoeur added to the sketch, the tragedy of the tortured Loyalist is lost, diminished to an unfortunate episode in a surely glorious war. Unmerited though his suffering is, his persecutors have a larger justice on their side.

The sketches that deal with the life of the farmer and the pattern of American society before the Revolution undergo a similar softening. "Reflections on the Manners of the Americans," that jaded version of the American success story in which the hero winds up materially wealthy and spiritually bankrupt, becomes the "Histoire de S. K.," the story of a settler who by virtue and diligence ends as the benevolent patriarch of the community he has founded in the wilderness. The realistic and rather troubled "Thoughts of an American Farmer on Various Rural Subjects" yields only two innocuous tales, the "Anecdote d'un Chien Sauvage" and the "Anecdote du Sassafras & de la Vigne Sauvage," both exercises in tender feelings and illustrations of the sweet fellowship of life in rural America. Even in those cases in which Crèvecoeur follows the outlines of the English prototype faithfully, he alters the tone and finally the significance of the sketch in translating it into French.

For example, the loveliest of the English sketches, "A Snow-Storm as It Affects the American Farmer," never quite loses touch with an earthy reality. The scene in which the farmer, having looked to his stock as the storm descends, enters his house is characteristic: "At last he returns home loaded with hail and snow melting on his rough but warm clothes; his face is red with the repeated injury occasioned by the driving wind. His cheerful wife, not less pleased, welcomes him home with a mug of gingered cider; and whilst she helps him to dried and more comfortable clothes, she recounts to him the successful pains she has taken also in collecting all her ducks, geese, and all the rest of her numerous poultry, a province less extensive indeed but not less useful" (*Sketches*, 43). The French version of the passage is as follows:

> Il revient enfin chez lui, non sans beaucoup de peine, marchant sur une couche de neige qui a déjà rempli les chemins. Ses habits simples, mais chauds & commodes, sont couverts de frimats & de glaçons; son visage, battu par le vent & les floccons de neige, est rouge & enflé. –Sa femme, ravie de le voir revenu avant la nuit, l'embrasse en le félicitant; elle lui offre une coupe de cidre mêlé avec du gingembre, & pendant qu'elle prépare les vêtemen[t]s dont elle veut qu'il se couvre, elle lui raconte les soins qu'elle a pris aussi de ses canards, de ses oisons & de toutes ses autres volailles. –Département moins étendu, à la vérité, mais non moins utile. (I, 298)

In part, the differences between the two passages stem from the fact that, although Crèvecoeur was well acquainted with rural

English, his re-education in French was confined to the language of the salons. But in the passage from the *Lettres* the controlling mentality, as well as the diction, is marked by an elegant conventionality, more concerned with balance and grace than with force and precision. And most of all, one regrets that the farmer and his wife are forced into highly sentimental and highly improbable attitudes. One can believe that in these circumstances an American farm wife might offer her husband a mug of gingered cider and dry clothes, but her rapture and her congratulatory embrace belong to the verse tales of Saint-Lambert rather than to the rigors of a Mohawk Valley winter.

Only about a half of the contents of the final, three-volume edition of the *Lettres* are reworkings of English originals. Although the remainder were written specifically for the new book, they are, if anything, still more diverse and incoherent than the materials Crèvecoeur salvaged from his English manuscripts. He seemingly ransacked every available source in order to fill out the pages of the *Lettres*: his own experience as a captive of the British in New York, stories that he had picked up from his fellow prisoners, anecdotes that he had collected from the newspapers, reports that he had compiled for his superiors in the foreign office —anything and everything was grist for his mill so long as it related to America and was in consonance with the preconceptions that the *Lettres* was designed to support. As a consequence, the new materials vary widely in interest and in literary value. Some are no more than reprints of public documents and addresses. Others are firmly conceived expository essays or fully developed narratives of individual experience, comparable in originality and vigor to the best of the English writings.

The least interesting pieces are those which cater most directly to the particular concerns of the French audience. Although the account of Washington's triumphal entrance with his army into New York City in 1783 has considerable historical value because Crèvecoeur was a witness to it, the other material on Washington and the letters which deal with Franklin and Lafayette are exclusively ceremonial in substance and adulatory in tone—sops to the French enthusiasm for the celebrities of the American Revolution. The new material on Quakers and on Indians also seems to be included for the sake of its readymade appeal. The letters on the Quaker notables Warner Mifflin and Anthony Bénézet reinforce the simplicity, humanitarianism, and courageous pacifism which the visit to Bartram and the Nantucket series emphasize. But the Indian in the English manuscripts is an indistinct and ambiguous figure, at times a boon companion and at others a merciless slaughterer. The additions to the *Lettres* introduce a wholly new image of the red man, that of the Ossianic hero—melancholy, grand, and nobly eloquent. Where the English manuscripts had glimpsed the Indian only through white eyes, the *Lettres* offer what pretend to be direct quotations of Indian discourse. One hears the speech of Lackawané as he denounces before the tribal council the proposal that the Indians adopt the agricultural ways of the whites, and one is permitted to overhear King Philip vow eternal resistance to the English as he converses with his aged adviser Siccacus. All the Indians of the French additions are gifted with an extraordinary capacity for metaphoric statement, all are steeped in the pathos of their inevitable extinction and frozen in attitudes of statuesque dignity—all are model embodiments of the clichés of eighteenth-century primitivism.

If the Indians of the *Lettres* are reduced to a stilted lifelessness, the figure of the author in the autobiographical letters is charged with an emotionality that borders on frenzy. He is forever the man of feeling, touched and moved, shuttled from one intense emotional state to another, each of which manifested in the gestures of weeping, praying, or embracing. But it is probably a mistake to view the self-portrait as a mere exercise in the school of sensibility. Surely the portrait is one that readers of Rousseau could appreciate, but its general accuracy is confirmed by the evidence of Crèvecoeur's private correspondence and by the observations of those who were acquainted with him. The autobiographical sections of the *Lettres* undoubtedly contain certain falsifications and suppressions, for one is never told of Crèvecoeur's Loyalist sympathies and very little of the circumstances of his wife's death or of his own response to it.

But, if ever a man lived the life of sensibility, it was Crèvecoeur. We know, moreover, that the experiences which the *Lettres* recount—the ordeal of imprisonment in New York and the threat to the safety of his children—were marked by an anxiety more intense than any he suffered during a lifetime punctuated by long periods of strain and uncertainty. The problem remains, however, that although the psychic revelations of the *Lettres* may be authentic, they afford only brief and meaningless glimpses into a life and a consciousness which the book otherwise obscures and disguises. Their place is in a sustained autobiography, one that might give them a context and a significance. In the *Lettres*, they come as startling intrusions, sudden appearances of the real Crèvecoeur amid the wooden Indians, representative settlers, and great men who populate the book.

When Crèvecoeur turns from his own wartime experiences to those of other and more typical victims of the Revolution, he regains the control and narrative clarity which distinguish such English sketches as the "History of Mrs. B." or "The American Belisarius." Here, of course, the emphasis is upon the atrocities of the English and the heroic sufferings of the embattled American Patriots, but the themes of the evil of *all* violence and the universal tragedy of a civil war are never quite lost. Whether Crèvecoeur actually acquired these stories from his fellow prisoners in New York, as the *Lettres* pretends, or whether some of them are the products of his imagination, is unimportant. The prison is an effective literary device, for it permits the author to assemble a gallery of representative victims of British oppression and furnishes a natural setting for their grim tales. In these narratives and in the other Revolutionary anecdotes in the *Lettres*, Crèvecoeur concentrates his attention on the texture of life in a civil war, a fearful existence of midnight arrests and unfounded charges, of sudden death and unsuspected betrayals. By the sheer weight of their numbers, as well as by the effectiveness of their presentation, the Revolutionary War stories create a sense of a world gone mad, a world for which the fitting image is the dark and rat-infested prison.

Powerful though the Revolutionary narratives are in their collective effect, individually they represent no significant advance beyond the war sketches among the English manuscripts. The major new achievement of the French writings is in a very different vein, the descriptive survey. Only in the Nantucket series do the *Letters* attempt a systematic delineation of the history, the economic and political organization, and the customs and manners of a segment of American society. But a principal effort of the *Lettres* is to describe the whole face of America, to report on the distinctive characteristics of each of its major regions, to probe its history in order to trace lines of social evolution, to measure the rate and chart the course of its progress in the arts and sciences. Thus the *Lettres* is, in fact, what the *Letters* is sometimes erroneously said to be: a detailed and sweeping survey of American civilization and its setting. James's observations are spotty and impressionistic; St. John's, comprehensive and informative.

Undoubtedly the new approach to the subject of America that the *Lettres* takes is a consequence of the duties and concerns which Crèvecoeur's role as consul thrust upon him. Howard Rice has suggested that the region-by-region survey of the Eastern seaboard in Volume II is adapted from the report that Crèvecoeur prepared for de Castries in 1783,[2] and the elaborate essays at the end of Volume III on the state of civilization in the new republic surely are reworked from materials that Crèvecoeur sent back to his superiors. But Crèvecoeur's early career as a cartographer and surveyor and his lifelong penchant for travel seem to indicate that the talent for observation, the eager curiosity, and the delight in comparative analysis which the *Lettres* displays were ingrained.

The virtues of the descriptive surveys in the *Lettres* are primarily expositional and analytical rather than imaginative and esthetic; and, as exposition and analysis, their forte is comprehensiveness. They take the reader on excursions into the seventeenth-century past of New England, supplying along the way the anecdote of the Regicide on which Hawthorne based "The Grey Champion." They pause to comment on the white pines of Maine, the Calvinism of Massachusetts, the Blue Laws of New Haven, the scenery along the Hudson, the roads of New Jersey, and the public institutions of Philadelphia. They lead one into the wilderness of the Ohio region and down the settled shores of the Connecticut. They are equally concerned with the lofty combat of an eagle and a fish hawk and with a new kind of boiler invented by Joseph Brown of Providence. They speculate on the psychological damage inflicted by the war and seek to account for the burgeoning technology of America by reference to the absence of traditions and precedents and to the high price of American labor.

The facts are not always reliable—the *Lettres* solemnly assures us that Boston was founded by a splinter group from Plymouth under the leadership of Cotton Mather—but they are plentiful and vivid; and, from the accumulated pattern which they form, emerges the external world that had remained shadowy and fragmentary in the *Letters*, the world of cities and mountains, of struggling colleges and booming shipyards, of Philadelphian astronomers and Hartford poets. The *Lettres* represents the first attempt by any commentator, European or American, to swallow America whole and to digest it. If for no other reason, it deserves attention as a worthy forerunner of the great surveys of Tocqueville and Bryce.

The reader of the *Lettres* comes away with the feeling that the skeleton of a coherent and meaningful work is in the book. The dungeon world of the Revolutionary pieces and the sunny vistas of the descriptive surveys suggest (but never quite articulate) a large and important statement about the essential polarities of the American experience and of universal human nature that is more fully objectified and wider in its view than the meanings of the *Letters*. Given the time and energy, freed from the necessity of fashioning the book as a support for his precarious career, Crèvecoeur might have succeeded in investing that skeleton with flesh and life. As it was, he was not to return for more than a decade to the task that the *Lettres* had left marred and unfinished.

II *America Once More*

If the *Lettres* is a book that reflects the accomplishment of one revolution, Crèvecoeur's last major work, *Voyage dans la Haute Pensylvanie et dans l'état de New-York*, is no less conditioned by the completion of another. Written in the closing years of the eighteenth century and in the first year of the nineteenth, the *Voyage* was published in Paris in 1801 as France, emerging from the shadow of a decade of turmoil and terror, looked to the young Napoleon as the restorer of order and peace. Crèvecoeur, silent during that decade, could breathe again; but the atmosphere was not yet untroubled. The words which he puts in the mouth of a friend in the preface to the new book describe the state of his mind at the time: "Freed from the chaos and horror of one of the most appalling revolutions that has ever drenched our land in blood, in fear and trembling even now at the memory of those laws of exile, expropriation, servitude, and disgrace, from which by a miracle the vision and courage of a young man (Napoleon Bonaparte) of thirty-one has just delivered us, we are now like the sailor who watches with mingled feelings of fright and gratitude from the harbor he has safely entered the reefs he has had the good fortune to avoid" (xvi).

With this mixture of renascent hope and lingering anxiety, Crèvecoeur turned once again to the matter of America, encouraged, perhaps, by the momentary revival of French interest in the United States that Napoleon's attempt to put on the mantle of Washington had stimulated, despite the years of strained relations between the two countries. But, though the subject is America, the France of the Revolution is never very distant; it haunts the book as an explicit threat to the political serenity of the New World and as the veiled specter of violence that darkens its otherwise sunny pages.

Abandoning the epistolary form in the *Voyage,* Crèvecoeur turns to another novelistic structural convention: the imaginary journey. The book pretends to be a translation of a battered manuscript, washed ashore from a shipwreck off Heligoland and rescued from destruction by the present editor and translator, who is identified on the title page as the author of the *Lettres d'un Cultivateur Américain.* The identity of the writer of the manuscript, of course, is a mystery; the initials S. J. D. C. offer the only clue, a sufficient one to readers of the *Lettres.* The device of the mysterious manuscript is an ancient one; but, as Crèvecoeur uses it, it is not merely an empty convention. It serves the very practical purpose of accounting for the strange organization of the book, for the supposed lacunae and problematical sequence of the battered papers free the author to range as he wishes. Because of its frequent use in eighteenth-century fiction, moreover, the device immediately establishes certain essential assumptions and expectations in the mind of the reader: the work is not to be merely the literal record of actual observations but is to be an act of the imagination as well, the validity of which is not to be measured in terms of the quantity and accuracy of its information but by its capacity to order and illuminate experience.

The *Voyage* is nearly without an external plot. The narrator, usually in the company of his young German friend Gustave Herman, wanders back and forth across the United States inspecting its celebrated natural features, attending Indian tribal councils, taking down the life histories of settlers and ironmongers, and interviewing well-known authorities on a variety of American topics. The role that he plays is far more passive than that of James in the *Letters;* rarely the actor, he is incessantly the witness, recorder, and commentator. As a result, the *Voyage* is filled with the clamor of different voices, each telling its story or offering its special viewpoint; there are literally scores of speakers in the book—hermits, politicians, Indians, exiled Portuguese royalty, academicians, and even the venerable Benjamin Franklin. Over all the scenes and conversations that constitute the texture of the book, the narrator presides as *raisonneur,* appraising, interpreting, and annotating what he sees and hears. As a character, he is virtually faceless. One knows that he has long been resident in America, that he has three sons and a daughter, that he is immensely proud of having been adopted years ago by the Oneida Indians, and that he is familiar with Europe and the Near East. But beyond that, he is simply the reasonable man, the selective intelligence through which the images and ideas of the world of the *Voyage* are developed.

His companion, Mr. Herman, is a more sharply defined personality. The son of a wealthy Hamburg merchant, he has come to the United States to further his education by travel and to attend to his family's business. A very romantic young man, he is attracted by the idea of primitive life and thrilled by the thought of Gothic antiquity. In the first half of the book particularly, he displays a marked tendency to overreact to what he sees and hears. Although the narrator forever urges moderation and restraint, Herman's comic enthusiasm sends the young man up a tree to catch an early glimpse of the next scenic wonder or leaves him swept by the arguments of the most recent speaker. Impressionable, naïve, eager, Herman is the initiate; and, insofar as the *Voyage* has a plot, it is the story of his initiation.

The setting of that initiation is America, but the wisdom which it imparts is universal in its application. Under the tutelage of the narrator and of wise men like Mr. G., the gentleman-farmer of New Jersey who delivers the peroration of the book, Herman sheds his illusions and confronts the vexing problems of man's innate moral nature, the rival claims of freedom and order, the limitations of human reason, and the other huge issues which the tour of America raises but for which it provides no neat solutions.

If the tendency of Herman's education in the New World is metaphysical, its daily content is made up of solid facts—the data and specifications of the commerce, agriculture, industry, and sociopolitical organization of the United States in the decade following the Revolution. Like the *Lettres*, but with far more system and clarity, the *Voyage* attempts to picture the whole fabric of life in the United States from New England to the South, from the established cities of the seaboard to the wilderness beyond the Alleghenies. In the course of their travels, the narrator and Herman seek out and question experts on land division and settlement, on Indian customs and manners, on foundries, on swamp-drainage, and on a host of other topics.

What the experts omit, the narrator supplies, either in the body of the book or in the massive array of notes that form one of the most curious features of the *Voyage*. The random facts and anecdotes that clutter the pages of the *Lettres* are here confined to the narrator's annotations, delightfully leisurely excursions through the bypaths of Crèvecoeur's eclectic concerns. If the tail sometimes wags the dog—the notes to the dedication are at least fifteen times longer than the text they serve—the reader is nevertheless free to browse through the notes as he will, for the body of the book stands without them; but he skips over them at his peril. The information that they convey is steadily fascinating in its scope and detail, embracing descriptions of the flora and fauna of America, biographies of eminent citizens, capsule accounts of towns and rivers, observations on agricultural and industrial techniques, remarks on Indian language and culture, definitions of Americanisms like *piazza* and *clearing*, and complete little essays on such topics as the Gulf Stream and the bones of the mammoth. For Crèvecoeur's contemporary audience, it must have been interesting to learn the details of the construction of a log cabin and that "nothing is bleaker than these log houses, when they suggest neither the idea of industry nor of cleanliness" (178, n. 5). For the modern reader, the notes often take on a certain poignancy, as does the description of a long-gone Newark as "a veritable Flora and Pomone" in the beauty of its gardens and orchards (603, n. 6).

But the depiction of the towns, institutions, and industries of the settled East is only one of several focal points in the descriptive passages of the *Voyage*. Of the others, the geographical descriptions and accounts of American scenery receive the least space and are remarkable chiefly for the new attention Crèvecoeur pays in them to the element of sublimity in nature. Scenic grandeur and the capacity of nature to inspire the thrill of terror are found only rarely in the earlier works,[3] for their main concern is with animate nature and that on the small scale of reptiles, birds, and insects. But in the *Voyage* Crèvecoeur dwells on the titanic landscape of Niagara and the imposing valley of the Hudson River, before which the narrator and his companion savor the sensations of sublimity and the impressions of vastness and age.

A related strand of Romanticism runs through portions of the Indian materials in the *Voyage*, the third major area of expository information in the book. Like the *Lettres*, the *Voyage* furnishes abundant examples of Indian eloquence; and, when Crèvecoeur allows his Indians to speak for themselves in ceremonial speeches, in conversation, and in what pretend to be transcriptions of Indian legends, they are noble savages indeed, fit companions of the Ossianic Indians of the *Lettres*.[4] But, when Crèvecoeur views the Indian through the eyes of the narrator or of one of the several white authorities on Indians who offer their testimony, the tone is apt to be less exalted, either dryly factual or explicitly anti-Romantic.

No matter what the tone, however, the Indian is a figure of extreme importance in the *Voyage*, occupying well over a quarter of the text and notes. In part, Crèvecoeur's concern with the Indian is simply expository, an effort to gratify the interest of his audience in an exotic subject of long-standing appeal; but it is also clear that, in the repeated debates and speculations on the relative merits of the hunting culture of the Indians and the settled agriculture of the white, in the several attempts to use the example of Indian life as a means of distinguishing the inborn nature of man from his acquired characteristics, and in the Job-like questioning of the divine plan to which the red men of the *Voyage* are addicted, the Indian is not only the focus of factual information but a major vehicle of Crèvecoeur's thematic concerns.

Much the same thing can be said of the last major body of subject matter in the *Voyage*, the seemingly endless series of inspections of new settlements and interviews with their pioneer inhabitants. Surely these passages and their notes supply an enormous amount of information about the techniques of clearing and farming new land and about the devices and institutions by which a community is organized and made to prosper in the wilderness. But most of that information is conveyed by the time one has accompanied the two travelers on their fifth or sixth visit to the backwoods. What is new on each occasion, however, is the background of experience and the particular attitude toward life of the settler. Each one contributes not only to the exposition of America and to the processes by which it is civilized but, more importantly, to a continuing dialogue on the errors and evils of the Europe from which most of the settlers have come and on the various benefits of a simple and agrarian existence. Again, as in the passages that deal with the Indians, the tendency of Crèvecoeur's implications is toward issues which transcend the limits of his American setting.

The *Voyage* is of unquestionable documentary value. As Percy G. Adams has pointed out, the book gives an extraordinarily early and full account of the phases of settlement and furnishes an important, if neglected, source for historians of the American frontier.[5] The *Voyage* would seem to be equally important to (and neglected by) students of American manufacturing, for Crèvecoeur's lively interest in inventions and mechanical processes results in detailed sketches of the state of technology in the United States on the eve of industrialization. The information on the frontier and American technological developments carries a particular authority because most of it is the product of Crèvecoeur's own observations. Professor Adams has ably demonstrated, however, that Crèvecoeur compiled the bulk of his Indian materials and the information on the northern Middle West from such published sources as the writings of William Bartram, Gilbert Imlay, William Smith, Thomas Jefferson, Jonathan Carver, and perhaps John Long, and, oddly, not from the authorities to which he attributes much of those materials: Benjamin Franklin, George Croghan, Frederick Hazen, Richard Butler, and Bernard Romans.[6]

Concerned though Crèvecoeur was to conceal the tracks of his research, he nevertheless made a significant new departure in the *Voyage* by this systematic use of factual sources which, with the exception of the often unreliable Carver, were among the very best available to him. Portions of the earlier writings were influenced by Crèvecoeur's reading—the impact of Raynal upon the *Letters* is the most conspicuous example—but none of them depends so heavily as the *Voyage* does on borrowings from specialists in particular fields of knowledge. The adoption of the new method is one more evidence of the effort to achieve completeness and authoritative accuracy in the depiction of America that is manifested throughout the *Voyage*.

III *The Imaginary Journey*

If the *Voyage*, with its great mass of information and its maps and statistical tables, represents Crèvecoeur's most ambitious attempt to document the society and geography of the United States, it is, at the same time, a book which works steadily in the direction of metaphysical statement; in the manner of imaginative literature rather than of reportage and analysis, it tends to convert its solid facts and specifications into images and symbols. Thus the *Voyage* at once heaps up the data of a literal reality and suggests to its reader that the data, in itself, is of little importance, that it represents only the momentary surface ripplings of huge enigmatic groundswells, the true concern of the book. As the book musters its authoritative spokesmen—Croghan, Franklin, and the rest—and accumulates its circumstantial detail, it simultaneously urges one by a variety of devices and techniques to view the elaborate panorama of Indians and farmers, of forests and towns as an illusion, a fantasy that has the oblique and disturbing import of dream.

The introductory business involving the sea-battered manuscript is one such device, but the principle one is the imaginary travel narrative that serves as the framework of the book. Realistic though many portions of that narrative are, its general shape and tenor are those of the account of a dream-journey. It is impossible, for example, to reconstruct with any degree of precision the chronology of the travels of the narrator and Mr. Herman; for time in the *Voyage* is elastic and looping. The earliest date mentioned as present time in the book is 1785, and the latest date cited in the notes is 1799; but the sequence of events within those limits is baffling. The first chapter of the initial volume is dated 1785, the second 1787, and the third, in which the narrator first acquires Herman as his traveling companion, is presumably set in 1788 or 1789, the dates which Crèvecoeur later gives for the great Indian council that the two set out to attend. Time moves continuously through the few months that the next nine chapters span, but then jumps to 1791, the date assigned to Chapter XIV. No new sequence is thereby established, however, for the following chapter returns us to 1790.

Time references are so vague in the second volume that it is impossible to establish the dates of the travels recounted there. The third volume is more specific but equally bewildering. The opening chapter consists of the autobiographical statement of Juan de Braganza, promised by his son, whom the travelers had interviewed in the second volume. Chapter II returns to an unspecified present time which carries continuously through the next two chapters. Chapter V pauses for a letter of 1786 from General Butler. With a few minor interruptions and jumps in time, the travel narrative resumes in Chapter VI and continues until the end, all the action taking place in the year 1798.

The itinerary of the tour is as confusing as its chronology. With each temporal shift, the reader is transported abruptly to a new locale, finding that the narrator whom he has left, perhaps, chatting with his host in the vicinity of Niagara has suddenly reappeared at a watering spot in the mountains of Virginia. The letters and interpolated tales which are spaced throughout the book intensify the sense of movement and dislocation by moving the reader still more violently in time and space, sometimes wrenching him backward thirty or forty years or wafting him without warning to European locales. But perhaps the eeriest effect of the discontinuities in the narration is that produced by the startling introduction of an unfamiliar and often unidentified speaker. The very first sentence of the book establishes the pattern: " 'What a vast subject for speculation the old and new inhabitants of North America offer!' continued Colonel Crawghan" (9). Again and again throughout the *Voyage*, figures loom up from the void and discourse; if one is lucky, a signature at the end of the chapter names the writer of the report, or a clue dropped in the course of the remark reveals his identity; if not, one is left to wonder.

On first encounter this peculiar method of the *Voyage* seems nothing more than the product of sheer clumsiness or of an absolute indifference to the conventions of narration. But, as one enters fully into the world of the book, the circling, shifting line of the narrative takes on a strange appropriateness. Reinforced by the timeless, fantastic quality of the several fables which Crèvecoeur offers in the guise of Indian legends and by the steady play of reference to dreams and dreamlike experiences, the shifting gives the action of the *Voyage* an inward and metaphoric impetus.

If the reader accepts the invitation of these suggestions to view the *Voyage* in one of its many aspects as a symbolic rather than a realistic journey, he can perceive that the essential chronology of the book is not the muddle of dates which mark the literal travels of the narrator but a simple and massive tripartite time scheme that centers on the highly developed societies of Europe, the nascent civilization of white America, and the primitive culture of the Indian. All three co-exist, of course, within the literal time span of the book; and each is touched upon by the experience of the two travelers. But, from the central viewpoint of the American narrator, the three phases take on the chronological sequence of future, present, and past. Thus Europe in the *Voyage* serves to supply an image of things to come; it represents a civilization in decline, a system in which innovation and the quest for perfection have at least become destructive forces, productive only of an anarchic collapse. Like the Europe of the *Letters*, it is crowded, corrupt, and oppressive, but here it is also a Europe in the grip of revolution, brought to the edge of chaos by "the most dangerous" of all manias, "that of perfection in Governments" (372). For the European, America offers the chance for a return to a simpler and more stable order of life, a refuge from the "convulsive storms of a disorganized society" (341), but to the

American Europe constitutes a grim forecast of his own future; the New World is "not far enough from Europe to prevent a volcanic explosion of new opinions which are spreading there; to prevent the impact of a background of cannon and victories from reaching" its shores (239).

The new republic exists in a precarious poise, threatened by the pull of the new ideas of revolutionary Europe and subjected to the retrogressive lure of the primitive wilderness. For in the *Voyage* the savage life of the forest exerts a real and dangerous charm. Its proponents, both red and white, regard it not only as man's natural state but as his most desirable one, an abandonment of the ambitious schemes, the unwarranted pride of reason, and all the artificial demands and restrictions to which they attribute human evil and misery. Example after example of whites who have succumbed to the attraction of the free life of the Indians seems to indicate "that the forests were the early cradle of human nature, that this innate taste, stifled by social education awaits only favorable circumstances for its manifestation" (471). For those who hold a darker view of primitive life, this attraction seems purely destructive, an atavistic impulse to retreat into a subhuman existence ungraced by intellect and imagination and incapable of achieving the harmony and stability of a settled society.

And, in the eyes of the anti-primitivists, to whom the narrator adds his considerable authority, the essential evil of an Indian existence is its violence: the inevitable bloodiness of hunting, the perpetual state of tribal warfare, the appalling cruelty of Indian tortures, and above all the addiction of primitive man to cannibalism. Although cannibalism was never in reality a conspicuous feature of Indian culture, it becomes in the *Voyage* a recurrent theme, the issue on which nearly every debate between savagery and civilization turns. To Crèvecoeur, it represents the ultimate horror—the last descent into evil of which man is capable. It is the original sin of the *Voyage,* the only act which even the beasts refuse, and the one from which man must be rescued at any cost.

Thus revolutionary Europe and the forests of the Indian are strangely linked. Both offer the promise of freedom, and both lead to violence and chaos. More importantly, both the primitivist and the revolutionary are deluded by a false conception of human nature. The primitivist's benign view of the life of the forest is predicated on the notion that, as an aged missionary priest expresses it, the Indians, "like other men . . . are born good, and of mild temperament" (289). Similarly, the maniacal quest of the revolutionist for institutional perfection is, according to the wise observer Mr. Duwitt, "founded on the alleged dignity of human nature" (507). And from both reversion and revolution, the stable and creative pattern of life in the new United States provides a safeguard, transient and fragile though it may be. The general view of American society in the *Voyage* is approximately the same as that developed in the first half of the *Letters*; in spite of the growth of commerce and industry since the war, in spite of affluence and independence, the country is still characterized by its order, simplicity, economic opportunity, and mild government. What is new in the *Voyage* is the attempt to place American society within the cycle of history: to account for it and to celebrate it by reference to the savage wilderness which it has overcome and the explosive disintegration which it has thus far avoided.

Given this huge three-phased time scheme, the journey to America, undertaken by Europeans like Mr. Herman and the many immigrants whom he and his guide interview, represents a voyage back in time, a return to a golden age long passed from the European experience. And, for both Herman and the American narrator, the journey into the wilderness is a still deeper exploration of the past, a probing of origins that is half-idyll, half-nightmare. For all the noble pathos and exotic appeal of the Indians and the sublimity of wild nature, the deepest penetration of the two travelers into the primitive past ends with their terrified recoil to civilization. The most powerful development of this aspect of the *Voyage* comes at the approximate midpoint of the work, the third chapter of Volume II.

There the narrator and Mr. Herman, touring the new settlements of the Juniata Valley in central Pennsylvania, decide to amuse themselves by going on a bee hunt in the forest that adjoins their host's farm. Setting out "in high spirits," they follow the trail their host has blazed into the wilderness, only to find themselves halted in less than half an hour by an impassable ravine, the very "reflection of destruction and ravage" (243). Disregarding the ominous import of the snake-filled pools and the jumble of fallen trees, they skirt the ravine and, in doing so, lose their way. Night overtakes them still astray; having lost their flint, they are unable to kindle a fire; and in the darkness Herman lies sleepless, listening to the sounds of the nocturnal forest, a victim of the terrifying "effect of darkness on the minds . . . of men" (245). Their confusion deepens during the next day as they search in vain for the path and for food, and the pangs of anxiety and hunger intensify.

That night they awake to a despair that has become rage, angrily heaping recriminations upon each other: "These passions, which until that moment we had never known, manifested themselves suddenly with the greatest violence, as if some evil jinn had suddenly blown them into our hearts. But no, the seeds that Nature had hidden there, were awaiting the distressing circumstance to which we had been reduced for full fruition before maturation. Ah! if in these dreadful moments, we had had weapons, or even the strength to seize one another, frantic as we were, one of us would certainly have killed the other" (246).

The fourth day finds them close to death, so weak that their eyes, "covered with the shadow of death, instead of seeing real objects, no longer saw anything but fantastic shapes as we lay agitated and trembling" (247). Prevented from committing suicide by the narrator, Herman urges his companion to kill his dog for food. Forgetting his long affection for the dog and "seized by a feeling more violent even than anger" (248), the narrator is about to stab the animal when he discovers the leaves of a groundnut at his feet. The two men feed eagerly on the nourishing roots; and, just as their strength returns, they hear the sound of cowbells. Finding the herd, they follow the cattle to a clearing, nearly overcome with joy in "the sudden transition from darkness . . . to light"; for the narrator, it is the "day of my second birth" (251).

The episode is patently an eighteenth-century version of the journey into "the heart of darkness," a fearful passage into the primitive past. Deprived of the devices of civilization, the blazed trail and the fire-making flint, the two men gradually revert to a state of nature such as Rousseau had never imagined, a state foreshadowed by the chaos of the snake-ridden ravine that they first encounter. Anxiety and despair give way to fury, an unreasoning and uncontrollable animosity that has all the time lain dormant within them, hitherto repressed only by the teachings and habits of civilization. But for the narrator, the final horror comes at the moment when he had been about to slay his dog, for in retrospect the act seems to him a manifestation of the impulse toward cannibalism. In his sudden, compulsive decision to plunge his knife into his pet, he sees a possible explanation of the origins of cannibalistic practices among primitive peoples. But it is not merely a problem in anthropology: "what about me? Have I not touched the moment of becoming a man-eating being? Most certainly, since I was on the point of seizing on the flesh of someone whom I loved . . ." (249). From this descent into savagery, the return to civilization is indeed a rebirth, an emergence from darkness into light.

IV A Dialogue on Existence

The ordeal in the forest makes explicit what is only latent in much of the *Voyage*: on one level of the complex narrative, the travels through America are the symbolic medium of a journey into the interior of the self, an exploration of the obscure recesses and unknown impulses of one's own essential nature. But that voyage of discovery is not conducted only, or even chiefly, by means of the personal experiences of the narrator and his companion. The primary devices is the long series of interviews, letters, and interpolated narratives by which a virtual anthology of varying points of view and personal histories is assembled. In this respect, the *Voyage* takes on something of the content and method of the philosophical tale; for, like Johnson's *Rasselas* or Voltaire's *Candide*, it develops its meanings by exposing a party of travelers to a multitude of different interpretations of life as they are offered by the various characters encountered on the tour.

Crèvecoeur's particular philosophical concerns are most vividly set forth in an apologue, supposedly a Cherokee legend that had been recorded and translated in 1774 and that has come years later into the hands of the narrator. In the legend, the Manitou, the Indian deity, undertakes a tour of inspection of his creation. Transforming himself into a wolf, he joins a pack and is pleased to see that, although they suffer many hardships, the wolves flourish as a species. In a series of successive metamorphoses, he interviews each of the different kinds of animals, hearing complaints and delivering his advice and consolation. At last he assumes the form of man and is invited to share in a banquet of human flesh. Horror-stricken, Manitou hurries away and stumbles into a pitfall. At the bottom of the pit, he discovers another victim of the trap, the Indian Wabémat. In his responses to Manitou's questions, Wabémat pictures his life as an endless series of frustrations and disasters. His present plight, caught in a hunter's trap, is emblematic of the human condition as he has experienced it, a strange transmutation of the imagery employed in the *Letters* in the episode of the caged Negro.

The hunter who laid the trap liberates Wabémat and Manitou with great reluctance, and the two continue their conversation. The god defends his creation by contending that the gifts of intelligence and sensibility more than make up for man's physical vulnerability. He admits that men, in common with all other creatures, are subject to the rule of chance on earth; but, if human reason alone can suffer from the anticipation of disaster, it also is unique in its capacity to hope for reward in the afterlife. Still ignorant of his companion's divine identity, Wabémat remains unconsoled. He invites Manitou to share his wretched food, timidly and apologetically confessing that he is unable to bring himself to eat human flesh as the other members of his tribe do, or to take delight in warfare. Manitou, delighted by Wabémat's nonconformity, offers the Indian the choice of two rewards: eternal happiness after death or the immediate enjoyment of the greatest happiness possible in an earthly existence. When Wabémat chooses the latter, his guest reveals himself as the creator-god and tells the quaking Indian that the choice requires Wabémat to resign his human nature; the possession of reason is incompatible with happiness and serenity.

Wabémat's reverence for the god does not prevent him from responding with one last complaint: "Powerful as you are, why, in order to achieve happiness, must I lose my identity as a human being? Is it possible that your eternal decrees have ordered that man should never know happiness? You, the creator, the organizer of all matter, the soul and the support of the universe! Give heed to your own goodness and Wabémat and his brethren will be happy. Since before calling man from the void of life, you necessarily foresaw his destiny on earth, why didn't you provide him with . . ." (234). His speech is cut short, for he is transformed in mid-question into a beaver; his tortured reason is replaced by the mild, unquestioning light of instinct.

Wabémat's last words and their context describe the ground explored in the series of philosophical discourses to which the narrator and Mr. Herman are exposed in the course of their travels. One character after another takes up the central enigma of the legend, the apparent irreconcilability of happiness and human nature, and pursues its implications. Nearly all are old men, rich in experience and close to death. Some are ancient Indians, spokesmen for a stoic resignation to the misery of existence and to the extinction that is death; or they are skeptical questioners who, like Wabémat, ponder the enigma of God's attitude toward man. For them, the nature and purposes of God are utterly inscrutable, and the only proper goal for man is oblivion, a release from time and consciousness.

Although a few of the whites, like the sorrowful old man whom Herman meets in a New Haven inn, share this death-wish, most of them attempt to give their lives some meaning and purpose. Some, like the elder Juan de Braganza, turn to the study of nature as a means of discovering the divine will and the duty of man. Others, like Mr. Hazen, recommend a Quaker-like abandonment of metaphysical speculation and the adoption of a life of moral action. Mr. E., the owner of a prosperous plantation near Niagara Falls, turns to history in quest of the unknown causes that determine human experience and meanwhile cultivates his American garden.

The contrast between Mr. E.'s farm, an island of serenity and fertility, and the barren chaos of the Falls to the north implies the only response to the dilemma of man that the *Voyage* as a whole seems to authorize. At one point in their conversation, Manitou had assured Wabémat that someday man "will subdue the elements, cross the seas, whose storms he will learn how to brave, he will improve the land and make of it a delightful home. It will depend only on him to become the artisan of his own glory and happiness" (229). Embattled by the chaos without and by the primeval impulse toward violence within, some men are nevertheless capable of fulfilling Manitou's prophecy, men such as Mr. E. and the other agents of civilization whom the narrator of the *Voyage* serves as witness.

This is the perspective in which the disparate materials of Crèvecoeur's most complex work can be seen to touch and join together. In their various ways, all the Indians of the *Voyage* enact Wabémat's choice; for, by resisting any progress toward civilization and by seeking the goal of unconsciousness, they abdicate their humanity. The energetic American society that the two travelers survey in all its phases becomes a panorama of right action: the model of an existence devoted to creation and to the laborious attainment of order. The disintegration of European society under the impact of revolution is the fruit of a failure to recognize the tenuous circumstances of human existence, an arrogant denial of the fact that man at all times is poised on the edge of darkness. By contrast, the wise men of the *Voyage* have a vivid awareness of human limitations, of the terrible forces of chance and necessity, of the huge mysteries which surround every small certainty. The last of these philosophical spokesmen describes the thoughts that come to him as he sits beneath the cedars of his farm, survivors from the virgin forest that once covered the land:

> It is under their pleasant shade that I sometimes go to dream, to meditate on our destiny, on life, that eternal circle of vicissitudes; now of order, now of peace and good fortune, now of wars, misfortunes, disorders of all kinds; on that swift cycle from birth till death, annihilation, and reproduction. What was the past like, I have often asked myself, in the shadowy wave of which events, generations, centuries plunged themselves? Like the waters of rivers in the depths of the Ocean? And this future which is nothing before arriving, and which leaves us the very moment it arrives; toward which, however, our imagination transports us at every moment that we may pin on it our tiniest hopes? And the present— fleeting, like the wind that blows, and which we scarcely enjoy, before it is gone? Placed between these different points which surround and escape him relentlessly, what is man? (567)

But Mr. G. soon leaves "these presumptuous flights of [an] intellect whose feebleness will never be able to break its bonds" (p. 567-68); he returns to nature, to the contemplation of his farm and family, and to the burgeoning new society around him. Wabémat's last question remains unanswered in the *Voyage;* but, in the face of ignorance and pain, a *modus vivendi* emerges.

Few good books have suffered the misfortunes to which the *Voyage* has been subjected. Received with little enthusiasm by its French audience, it was left virtually unread throughout the remainder of the nineteenth century. The revival of interest in Crèvecoeur in the twentieth century ignored the *Voyage*, which was dismissed by the foremost student of Crèvecoeur as "une sorte d'épilogue" to the *Letters*.[7] Not until the 1940's did the book begin to receive serious consideration in the thoughtful studies of Percy Adams, and not until 1964 was it made again available to a wide audience; Clarissa Bostelmann's translation of that year was the first republication of the full text after the original edition of 1801. There is, of course, reason for that neglect: for, if the *Voyage* is a good book, it is also a difficult and demanding one. It is too long by far, repetitious and slow in its development. Its ornate and sometimes windy style is burdensome, and its top-heaviness is only exaggerated in translation. Its structure seems to be at odds with its ostensible purposes and is alone sufficient to put off the reader too impatient with eccentricity to perceive the method in Crèvecoeur's madness. But perhaps the cardinal sin of the *Voyage* is that it rebuffs the reader who values Crèvecoeur chiefly for his supposed artlessness and naïveté, for in none of his work are strategy and intellectual abstraction so evident as in this one.

For the most part, these flaws and impediments are consequences of Crèvecoeur's extreme ambition, the symptoms of strain which always accompany the attempt of a small, if authentic, talent to accomplish a great work. If one may compare a minor author to a major one, the *Voyage* shares certain qualities with Melville's *Mardi*, that desperate attempt to make a statement larger than the writer's art could convey, a book that is at once splendid and annoying. The wonder of the *Voyage*, however, is that it is not the product of a young writer who had momentarily outreached his developing abilities but the work of a man who was approaching the end of a career that had quite literally exhausted him. And yet everywhere in the book are the marks of a questing mind and an innovating art—everywhere the signs of life and growth.

CHAPTER 6

The Significance of Crevecoeur

THE PLACE of Crèvecoeur in social and intellectual history is fairly clear; the nature and the extent of his artistic achievement are still, however, in the process of being defined. The wide and careful research of Howard Rice has demonstrated beyond question that, in the crucial decade of 1785 to 1795, the American Farmer served as a major interpreter of America to Europe. Published in Dublin, Belfast, Leyden, Maastricht, Leipzig, and Berlin, as well as in London and Paris, Crèvecoeur's book shaped the idea of America in the minds of the Irish emigrant, the Parisian bluestocking, the German liberal, and the Dutch merchant.

Some, like Lezay-Marnézia and the other unhappy French colonists in Ohio, embraced the *Lettres* as an immigrant's guide, only to be bitterly disillusioned by the distance between Crèvecoeur's sentimental vignettes and the realities of frontier settlement. For reformers like Brissot and his fellow Girondists, the *Lettres* charted the course to a political and social utopia; for Romantics like Bernadin de Saint-Pierre and Chateaubriand, it confirmed the dream of a primitive America. Although Crèvecoeur's works were soon replaced by more up-to-date and reliable sources of information on the United States, his writings made their impress upon the European consciousness at a moment when interest in America was at its peak—the moment when the European image of America was caught and fixed. In any serious study of the American dream as it inhabited the imagination of Europe in the nineteenth century and beyond, Crèvecoeur must occupy a central position.[1]

Crèvecoeur seems, however, to have made no such impress on his English-speaking audience. Although the London editions of the *Letters* were widely reviewed and excerpts from them reprinted in several leading magazines, the book was subjected to a withering attack by Samuel Ayscough in 1783 as a fraudulent attempt to encourage emigration from the British Isles. In 1818, John

Bristed coupled Crèvecoeur and Gilbert Imlay as two writers who "have exceedingly exaggerated the excellencies of the United States, by representing them as the abode of *more* than all the perfection of innocence, happiness, plenty, learning, and wisdom, than *can* be allotted to human beings to enjoy,"[2] an opinion soon to be echoed by the poet Thomas Moore. Although the assertion is often made that the *Letters* exerted a profound influence on Coleridge and Southey at the time of their interest in "Pantisocracy," no evidence exists to indicate that either had ever read Crèvecoeur.[3] It seems that Mary Lamb's response in 1805 to William Hazlitt's recommendation that she read the *Letters* describes the general reputation of the book in Great Britain: "tell Hazlitt not to forget to send the *American Farmer*. I daresay it is not so good as he fancies; but a book's a book."[4]

In the United States, interest in the *Letters* faded even more quickly. During the period of Crèvecoeur's consulship, when he was a well-known figure in the country, his book received considerable attention. Episodes from it were widely reprinted in the magazines, and George Washington found the *Letters* to "afford a great deal of profitable and amusive information," but he feared that its picture of America was in some instances "embellished with rather too flattering circumstances."[5] But, by 1793, interest in Crèvecoeur had ebbed to the point that Matthew Carey's first American edition of the *Letters,* published in that year, was a financial failure. To Samuel W. Eager, whose history of the region near Pine Hill appeared in 1847, Crèvecoeur was an obscure if slightly exotic figure who "lived where Hezekiah Moffat, Esq. lived and died."[6] The more sophisticated Duyckinck brothers could identify him in their great *Cyclopaedia of American Literature* by comparing his work to Mrs. Grant's *Memoirs* for its antiquarian charm as an image of life in colonial America; the *Letters,* however, suffered in the comparison, for the book "is all sentiment and susceptibility in the French school of St. Pierre and Chateaubriand, looking at homely American life in the Claude Lorraine glass of fanciful enthusiasm." [7]

By the middle of the nineteenth century, in France as well as in England and the United States, Crèvecoeur was a half-forgotten figure from a past that was by now quaint. As the documentary value faded, the *Letters* became an obscure "curiosity of literature," known and cherished by a few discerning readers and neglected by the mass. To James Russell Lowell, the *Letters* was "a dear book, with some pages in it worthy of Selborne White";[8] but Lowell's opinion was testimony to the breadth of his own reading rather than to that of Crèvecoeur's reputation. In all the nineteenth century, only one significant attempt was made to claim for Crèvecoeur a place of importance in the ranks of American writers. Twenty-five years after Hazlitt had urged Mary Lamb to read the *Letters,* he took up the cause of the Farmer again in the pages of the *Edinburgh Review.* The occasion was a sweeping survey of American writing which the critic conducted under the pretense of reviewing William Ellery Channing's *Sermons and Tracts.*

After taking a rather jaded look at Irving, Brown, and Cooper, Hazlitt turned to three writers occupying "a higher and graver place in the yet scanty annals of American Literature": Franklin, Edwards, and "the author (whoever he was) of the *American Farmer's Letters.*" Of the three, the last received the most attention. In the *Letters,* Hazlitt found a demonstration of "how American scenery and manners may be treated with a lively, poetic interest," of how "not only the objects, but the feelings of a new country" may be rendered. But the chief virtue of the book was its lack of pretense and affectation, a virtue denied to most American writers "by the dread of being thought vulgar, which necessarily makes them so, or the determination to be fine, which must for ever prevent it." The unknown author of the *Letters,* however, possessed in abundance the "power to sympathize with nature, without thinking of ourselves or others," which, "if it is not a definition of genius, comes very near to it."[9] Hazlitt's high regard for the *Letters* was not confirmed by subsequent criticism until 1919, when another British student of American writers, D. H. Lawrence, included the book among his examples of classic American literature.

But Lawrence considered the *Letters* only after what Hazlitt had failed to bring about had been accomplished: the revival of a broadly based and many-faceted interest in Crèvecoeur. The chief agent of that revival was the publication in the United States of Ludwig Lewisohn's edition of the *Letters* in 1904 and in England of Warren Barton Blake's edition in 1912, the first reissues of any of Crèvecoeur's major works in more than one hundred years. Since 1912, Crèvecoeur's writings have been made still more widely available by the publication of two more popular editions of the *Letters*, the selections from the English manuscripts in the *Sketches*, and the recent translation of the *Voyage*. In 1916 Julia P. Mitchell published her full-scale biography of Crèvecoeur, a study which, in spite of a serious misconstruction of the evidence bearing on Crèvecoeur's early career, filled in many of the gaps left by its only predecessor, the family biography which Robert de Crèvecoeur had written some thirty years earlier. The French writings have been rescued from their long neglect by Howard Rice's detailed examination of the composition and influence of the *Lettres* and by Percy Adams' pioneering studies of the *Voyage*.

As a result of this sustained attention, Crèvecoeur's inclusion in any comprehensive anthology or history of American literature is now assured. But the precise nature and value of his contribution to that literature remains obscure. Is he to be grouped with the pamphleteers of the Revolutionary period as a social and political commentator? Are his writings chiefly significant as tokens of the early stirrings of Romanticism in America? Is he to be regarded as an autobiographer, a nature writer, a Tory propagandist, a foreign observer? Or is he to be accorded the status of a writer whose achievements are of interest in themselves, whose works by their force and complexity resist tidy categorization and demand to be approached on their own terms?

There are a number of reasons for the amorphousness of Crèvecoeur's present reputation. The traditional emphasis of the study of eighteenth-century American literature, one dominated by the figures of Edwards and Franklin, has been on its ideological and social implications rather than on its intrinsic value as art; Crèvecoeur's writings, forced to fit the mold, have been distorted in the process. When the literature of the century *is* approached as belles-lettres, the focus has been on the origin and development of the literary genres in America, a focus which has sharpened our understanding of the poetry of Freneau, the drama of Tyler, and the fiction of Brown but which has bypassed the work of Crèvecoeur, for most of his writings offer only analogies to the principles and strategies of the conventional genres. And to those who are concerned with the Americanness of American literature and who insist that English is its only proper tongue, Crèvecoeur is an anomaly, a summer visitor rather than a resident.

If Crèvecoeur's writings indeed represent the artistic achievement that the present study has claimed for them, his position in American literature is in urgent need of clarification and reassessment. From a perspective that embraces the entire body of that literature, Crèvecoeur is clearly not a major figure. Like every other writer of his period, he is dwarfed by the shapers of the American renaissance in the following century. But, within his own century, his importance is considerable. If he lacks the personal stature and cultural significance of Edwards and Franklin, his work exceeds theirs in intrinsic literary interest; it transcends, as their works often do not, the goals of persuasion and exposition and achieves the completeness and self-sufficiency of art. Against the background of the belletristic writings of the century, the *Letters* stands out, distinguished by those qualities of originality and esthetic honesty which Hazlitt found in the book. At Crèvecoeur's best, he succeeded in doing what has always been a rare achievement in American literature and what had proved particularly difficult in the formative years before 1800: he saturated his work in the characteristic imagery of the country and then transformed those materials of American experience into the metaphorical vehicles of meanings that radiate far beyond the limits of a particular time and place. In this respect, he is an American artist, one of the most powerful and versatile that his century produced.

And yet, like Freneau, Tyler, and Brown, like all the young men who undertook the pursuit of literature in eighteenth-century America, Hector St. John of Pine Hill was an artist *manqué*, a writer who was never permitted by the circumstances of his life to bring the promise of his early work to the fulfillment of artistic maturity. Caught by the pressure of events and thrust into an occupation and a milieu that separated him from the rural America which nourished his best perceptions, Crèvecoeur never recovered the poise and authority that he had attained in the *Letters*. It is impossible to guess what course his art might have taken if he had been able to stand his ground, whether it would have continued the movement toward fiction that is evident in the narrative of James or pursued any of the several intriguing paths explored in the *Sketches*. Surely he would not have felt the desire to court official favor that required him to pad and polish his earlier work as he did in the *Lettres*, nor would he have experienced the remoteness from his American materials that sent him on the metaphysical excursions of the *Voyage*.

But, if the natural development of his art was truncated, the vital source of that art is apparent in all his work: the deep and sustained awareness of the ambiguous nature of reality. In all his work, the depiction of serenity and freedom is qualified by the imagery of entrapment and anguish; one recalls the cage of Letter IX, the prison of the *Lettres*, the pitfall of the *Voyage*. In all his work there are, as Moses Coit Tyler long ago discovered in the *Letters*, "two distinct notes—one of great peace, another of great pain."[10] That double awareness, together with the tension and resonance of the accompanying response, does not in itself guarantee the creation of great art; but it seems a necessary prerequisite for great art. This quality we have come to admire in Edward Taylor and Jonathan Edwards, in the late Franklin, and in the early Freneau. Perhaps it is time that we recognized it in St. John de Crèvecoeur.

Notes and References

All page references to Crèvecoeur's major writings are made parenthetically in my text. I have used the following editions: *Letters from an American Farmer* (London, 1783); *Sketches of Eighteenth Century America* (New Haven, 1925); *Lettres d'un Cultivateur Américain*, 3 vols. (Paris, 1787); *Journey into Northern Pennsylvania and the State of New York*, trans. Clarissa S. Bostelmann (Ann Arbor, 1964).

Chapter One

1. From a letter written in 1785, quoted in French by Robert de Crèvecoeur, *Saint John de Crèvecoeur: Sa vie et ses ouvrages* (Paris, 1883), p. 5.

2. From an autobiographical sketch written in 1803, quoted in French by Robert de Crèvecoeur, p. 5.

3. So little is known of this episode in Crèvecoeur's life that Julia P. Mitchell in *St. Jean de Crèvecoeur* (New York, 1916) denies that he ever saw service in Canada and contends that he came directly to the British colonies from England. In *Sketches of Eighteenth Century America*, ed. H. L. Bourdin, R. H. Gabriel, and S. T. Williams, p. 15, Henri Bourdin establishes conclusively that the author of *Letters from an American Farmer* and the officer named Crèvecoeur who was obliged to resign from the Regiment de la Sarre in 1759 were one and the same.

4. A reproduction of this watercolor may be found in the *Pennsylvania Magazine of History and Biography*, XXX (1906), 257.

5. From a letter to Rochefoucauld, April 24, 1785, translated from the French and quoted by Mitchell, p. 144.

6. Mitchell, p. 8, believes that the sketch of a Gothic castle in *Voyage dans la Haute Pensylvanie et dans l'état de New-York* (Paris, 1801), I, Ch. XIV (*Journey*, pp. 105–13), is a sample of Crèvecoeur's juvenilia. According to Robert de Crèvecoeur, however, the sketch was written in 1796.

7. From a document in the records of the British Foreign Office, quoted in French by Mitchell, pp. 313–14.

8. See Howard C. Rice, *Le Cultivateur Américain: Étude sur l'oeuvre de Saint John de Crèvecoeur* (Paris, 1932), p. 19, n. 2.

9. From a letter of Henry Wisner to George Clinton, February 19, 1778, quoted by Mitchell, p. 47.

10. From a letter to Roger Morris, February 17, 1779, quoted by Mitchell, p. 50.

11. From a letter from Major-General James Pattison to Sir Henry Clinton, July 8, 1779, quoted by Mitchell, pp. 54–55.

12. James Boswell, *The Life of Samuel Johnson* (New York, 1931), p. 237.

13. From Crèvecoeur's note on the manuscript of the *Letters,* quoted by Robert de Crèvecoeur, p. 64, n. 2.

14. From a letter of August 10, 1781, translated from the French by Ludwig Lewisohn, ed., *Letters from an American Farmer* (New York, 1904), pp. 331–32.

15. From a letter of August 28, 1781, printed by Warren Barton Blake, ed., *Letters from an American Farmer* (London, 1912), pp. 236–37.

16. From a letter of September 26, 1781, printed by Blake, pp. 238–39.

17. From a letter of October 30, 1781, translated by Lewisohn, pp. 337–38.

18. From a letter of December 5, 1781, printed in Lewisohn, pp. 338–39.

19. From the manuscript "Souvenirs sur Mm. la comtesse d'Houdetot" (1813), quoted in French by Robert de Crèvecoeur, p. 71.

20. Samuel Breck, *Recollections*, ed. H. E. Scudder (Philadelphia, 1877), pp. 80, 81–82.

21. See the report of the Count de Moustier to the French ministry, quoted by Rice, pp. 35–36.

22. From the *Memoires,* quoted in French by Rice, p. 34.

23. See Robert de Crèvecoeur, p. 179.

24. Robert de Crèvecoeur, pp. 167, 196.

25. Rice, p. 44; Robert de Crèvecoeur, p. 279.

Chapter Two

1. See Crèvecoeur's letter of May 18, 1785, to Thomas Jefferson in *The Papers of Thomas Jefferson,* ed. J. P. Boyd (Princeton, 1953), VIII, 155–56.

2. See Rice, p. 111.

3. For a discussion of Quaker anti-slavery activity and of Crèvecoeur's interest in it, see Rice, pp. 109–11.

4. The scene of the caged Negro in Letter IX may derive from a phantasmagorial transmutation of the materials of the passage just quoted. The twenty-three-minute ordeal is lengthened into an agony of two days, the stake becomes the suspended cage, the mosquitoes

are transformed into birds-of-prey, and the remorseful Jersey farmer reappears as the arrogant Carolinian slavemaster.

5. It must be acknowledged, however, that Crèvecoeur is not entirely consistent on this (or any other) point. On occasion, he seems to espouse a rigid environmental determinism. He suggests, for example, that the simple and honest society of the inhabitants of the Hebrides "would present an interesting spectacle, could they be transported on a richer soil. But perhaps that soil would soon alter every thing; for our opinions, vices, and virtues, are altogether local: we are machines fashioned by every circumstance around us" (101). On the whole, however, Crèvecoeur refuses to restrict the possibilities of life in the New World to the limits defined by the physical setting. What distinguishes America from Europe is not its soil and climate but its political, economic, and cultural organization.

6. Paul H. Johnstone, "In Praise of Husbandry," *Agricultural History*, XI (1937), 94. For my discussion of the revival of interest in agriculture in the eighteenth century, I am indebted to this excellent article and to the same author's "Turnips and Romanticism," *Agricultural History*, XII (1938), 224–55.

7. [Hans Caspar] Hirzel, *The Rural Socrates* in [Arthur Young], *Rural Oeconomy: or, Essay on the Practical Parts of Husbandry* (Philadelphia, 1776), p. 173.

8. [Thomas-François-Guillaume] Raynal, *A Philosophical and Political History of the British Settlements and Trade in North America* (Edinburgh, 1779), p. 269.

9. Chester E. Eisinger, "The Freehold Concept in Eighteenth Century American Letters," *William and Mary Quarterly*, 3rd ser., IV (1947), 44.

10. Crèvecoeur regularly spells the naturalist's last name with an *e*.

11. See Rice, pp. 50–54.

12. H. N. Fairchild, *The Noble Savage: A Study in Romantic Naturalism* (New York, 1928), pp. 101–3.

13. Ralph H. Gabriel, "Crèvecoeur and His Times," in *Sketches of Eighteenth Century America*, p. 2.

14. Percy H. Boynton, *Literature and American Life* (Boston, 1936), p. 104.

15. For a discussion of the place of the *Letters* in the formulation of the American pastoral ideal, see Leo Marx, *The Machine in the Garden* (New York, 1964), pp. 107–16.

Chapter Three

1. *Correspondance littéraire, philosophique et critique par Grimm,*

Diderot, Raynal, Meister, etc., ed. Maurice Tourneux (Paris, 1880), XIV, 88.

2. Lewisohn, ed., *Letters from an American Farmer*, pp. xv–xvi; *Expression in America* (New York, 1932), p. 38.

3. D. H. Lawrence, *The Symbolic Meaning: The Uncollected Versions of Studies in Classic American Literature*, ed. Armin Arnold (Arundel, Eng., 1962), p. 60.

4. John Brooks Moore, "Crèvecoeur and Thoreau," *Papers of the Michigan Academy of Science, Arts and Letters*, V (1925), 321.

5. John Brooks Moore, "The Rehabilitation of Crèvecoeur," *Sewanee Review*, XXXV (1927), [216], 221.

6. See Marius Bewley, *The Eccentric Design: Form in the Classic American Novel* (New York, 1959), pp. 102–6.

7. See the Foreword by Albert E. Stone, Jr., to *Letters from an American Farmer and Sketches of Eighteenth-Century America* (New York, 1963), pp. vii–xxvi.

8. Stone, p. xxiv.

9. Gabriel, p. 10.

10. Letter III, for example, is supposedly written in 1778; Andrew had come to America in 1774, and his career over his first four years in the New World is traced. But neither that letter nor the ones that precede it give any indication of the bitter fighting that had been in progress for three years. Indeed, the first references to actual warfare do not appear until the last letter, which seems to allude to the guerrilla attacks led by Butler against the Pennsylvania frontier in the summer of 1778.

11. R. W. B. Lewis, *The American Adam: Innocence, Tragedy, and Tradition in the Nineteenth Century* (Chicago, 1955), p. 197.

12. See Enos Hitchcock, *The Farmer's Friend, or The History of Mr. Charles Worthy* (Boston, 1793), pp. 51–53.

13. D. H. Lawrence, *Studies in Classic American Literature* (New York, 1953), p. 37.

14. Raynal, pp. 243–44.

15. Lawrence, *Studies in Classic American Literature*, p. 37.

16. See James R. Masterson, "The Tale of the Living Fang," *American Literature*, XI (1939), 66–73.

17. See James R. Masterson, "Travelers' Tales of Colonial Natural History," *Journal of American Folklore*, LIX (1945–46), 51–67, 174–88.

18. See Laurence M. Klauber, *Rattlesnakes: Their Habits, Life Histories, and Influence on Mankind* (Berkeley and Los Angeles, 1956), I, 377; and II, 845, 1074–75, 1220–24, 1249–51.

19. Lawrence, *Studies in Classic American Literature,* p. 37.
20. Bewley, p. 105.

Chapter Four

1. *Letters from an American Farmer,* pp. v, vi.
2. I have followed Rice, pp. 229–30, in the dating of Crèvecoeur's English manuscripts.
3. The publication of *Sketches* was attended by an extensive campaign to alert readers to the nature and importance of the work. H. L. Bourdin and S. T. Williams beat the drums for their book in "The American Farmer Returns," *North American Review,* CCXXII (1925), 135–40, and in "The Unpublished Manuscripts of Crèvecoeur," *Studies in Philology,* XXII (1925), 425–32, and offered tantalizing samples of the newly discovered English writings in "Crèvecoeur, the Loyalist; The Grotto: An Unpublished Letter from The American Farmer," *Nation,* CXXI (1925), 328–30; "Crèvecoeur on the Susquehanna," *Yale Review,* XIV (1925), 552–84; "Hospitals (during the Revolution)," *Philological Quarterly,* V (1926), 157–65; and "Sketch of a Contrast between the Spanish and English Colonies," *University of California Chronicles,* XXVIII (1926), 152–63.
4. Moore, "The Rehabilitation of Crèvecoeur," pp. 223, 225.
5. See Rice, p. 142, n. 2.
6. See Mitchell, p. 45.
7. Cf. J[onathan] Carver, *Travels through the Interior Parts of North America . . .,* 3rd ed. (London, 1781), pp. 492–93.
8. Moore, "The Rehabilitation of Crèvecoeur," p. 228.
9. Stanley T. Williams, "Crèvecoeur as a Man of Letters," in *Sketches,* p. 31.

Chapter Five

1. Lacretelle's review is reprinted in *Lettres,* I, xv–xxxii.
2. See Rice, p. 83, n. 6.
3. Chief among the few examples are the sketch of the falls of the Connecticut in *Lettres,* III, 34–40, and the cave scenery of the English manuscript "The Grotto."
4. For a full discussion of Romantic elements in Crèvecoeur's treatment of the Indians and in the *Voyage* as a whole, see Percy G. Adams, "Crèvecoeur–Realist or Romanticist?" *French American Review,* II (1949), 115–35.
5. See Adams, "The Historical Value of Crèvecoeur's *Voyage . . .,*" *American Literature,* XXV (1953), 150–68, and *Crèvecoeur's Eigh-*

teenth-Century Travels in Pennsylvania & New York (Lexington, Ky., 1961), pp. xxiii–xxviii.

6. See Adams, "Crèvecoeur and Franklin," *Pennsylvania History*, XIV (1947), 273–79; "Notes on Crèvecoeur," *American Literature*, XX (1948), 327–33; and *Crèvecoeur's Eighteenth-Century Travels*, pp. xxxv–xli.

7. Rice, p. 103.

Chapter Six

1. For a compact and detailed discussion of Crèvecoeur's European influence, see Howard C. Rice, "Some Notes . . . on the American Farmer's Letters," *Colophon*, Pt. XVIII, No. 3 (1934).

2. John Bristed, *The Resources of the United States of America . . .* (New York, 1818), p. 4.

3. See Oliver F. Emerson, "Notes on Gilbert Imlay, Early American Writer," *PMLA*, XXXIX (1924), 427–31, and William Haller, *The Early Life of Robert Southey: 1774–1803* (New York, 1917), p. 123, n. 1.

4. Charles Lamb, *The Complete Works and Letters*, ed. Saxe Commins (New York, 1935), p. 748.

5. Quoted by W. P. Trent, Prefatory Note to *Letters from an American Farmer*, ed. Lewisohn, p. viii.

6. Samuel W. Eager, *An Outline History of Orange County . . .* (Newburgh, N. Y., 1846–47), p. 488.

7. Evert A. and George L. Duyckinck, *Cyclopaedia of American Literature* (New York, 1856), I, 173.

8. From a letter to E. L. Godkin, May 2, 1869, in *Letters of James Russell Lowell*, ed. C. E. Norton (New York, 1894), II, 30.

9. [William Hazlitt], rev. of W. E. Channing, *Sermons and Tracts*, *Edinburgh Review*, L (1829), 130–31.

10. Moses C. Tyler, *The Literary History of the American Revolution* (New York, 1897), II, 351.

Selected Bibliography

PRIMARY SOURCES

This bibliography is limited to Crèvecoeur's major published writings. For a full listing of the various reprintings and translations of the *Letters* and the *Voyage*, of Crèvecoeur's agricultural pamphlets and articles, and of his letters and manuscripts, see Rice, *Le Cultivateur Américain*, pp. 231–38.

Letters from an American Farmer. London: Davies and Davis, 1782.

Letters from an American Farmer. 2nd ed. London: Davies and Davis, 1783.

Lettres d'un Cultivateur Américain. 2 vols. Paris: Cuchet, 1784.

Lettres d'un Cultivateur Américain. 2nd ed. 3 vols. Paris: Cuchet, 1787.

Voyage dans la Haute Pensylvanie et dans l'état de New-York, 3 vols. Paris: Maradan, 1801.

Sketches of Eighteenth Century America. Ed. H. L. Bourdin, R. H. Gabriel, and S. T. Williams. New Haven: Yale University Press, 1925.

"Crèvecoeur on the Susquehanna, 1774–1776." Ed. H. L. Bourdin and S. T. Williams, *Yale Review*, XIV (1925), 552–84.

"The Grotto: An Unpublished Letter from The American Farmer." Ed. H. L. Bourdin and S. T. Williams. *Nation*, CXXI (1925), 328–30.

"Hospitals (during the Revolution): An Unpublished Essay by J. Hector St. John de Crèvecoeur." Ed. H. L. Bourdin and S. T. Williams. *Philological Quarterly*, V (1926), 157–65.

"Sketch of a Contrast between the Spanish and English Colonies." Ed. H. L. Bourdin and S. T. Williams, *University of California Chronicles*, XXVIII (1926), 152–63.

Journey into Northern Pennsylvania and the State of New York. Trans. Clarissa S. Bostelmann. Ann Arbor: University of Michigan Press, 1964.

SECONDARY SOURCES

This bibliography stresses the more recent and important biographical and critical studies of Crèvecoeur. Many other sources are cited in the footnotes. For listings of contemporary reviews of Crèvecoeur's writings, consult the books by Robert de Crèvecoeur, Julia Mitchell, and Howard Rice.

ADAMS, PERCY G. "Crèvecoeur and Franklin," *Pennsylvania History,* XIV (1947), 273–79. Investigates the sources of the materials assigned to Franklin in the *Voyage.*

————. "Crèvecoeur–Realist or Romanticist?" *French American Review,* II (1949), 115–35. Finds evidences in the *Voyage* of the influence of late eighteenth-century French Romanticism.

————. Introduction to *Crèvecoeur's Eighteenth-Century Travels in Pennsylvania & New York.* Lexington: University of Kentucky Press, 1961. Brings together the findings of the editor's earlier articles.

————. "The Historical Value of Crèvecoeur's *Voyage* . . .," *American Literature,* XXV (1953), 150–68. Discussion of the importance of the *Voyage* as a record of American society in the first decade of independence.

————. "Notes on Crèvecoeur," *American Literature,* XX (1948), 327–33. Analysis of the sources of the *Voyage.*

BLAKE, WARREN BARTON. Introduction to *Letters from an American Farmer.* London: Dent, 1912. Factually accurate and balanced survey together with a sampling from Crèvecoeur's correspondence with Franklin and Jefferson.

CRÈVECOEUR, ROBERT DE. *Saint John de Crèvecoeur: Sa vie et ses ouvrages.* Paris: Librarie des Bibliophiles, 1883. Dated and reticent, but still the fullest account of Crèvecoeur's personal life; prints a generous selection from his correspondence.

LAWRENCE, D. H. *Studies in Classic American Literature.* New York: Doubleday, 1953. Pp. 31–43. Provocative and sometimes inaccurate approach to the *Letters* as a work divided between authentic insight and artificial sentiment (first published in 1923).

————. *The Symbolic Meaning,* ed. Armin Arnold. Fontwell, Arundel: Centaur Press, 1962. Pp. 53–70. Earlier, longer, more thoughtful version of the essay in *Studies in Classic American Literature* (first published in 1919).

LEWISOHN, LUDWIG. Introduction to *Letters from an American Farmer.* New York: Fox, Duffield, 1904. Marred by factual inaccuracies but significant as an early attempt to define the literary value of the *Letters;* selections from Crèvecoeur's correspondence with Franklin are printed in an appendix.

MITCHELL, JULIA P. *St. Jean de Crèvecoeur.* New York: Columbia University Press, 1916. Unreliable in its treatment of Crèvecoeur's early life, but supplies the fullest account of his activities as consul.

MOORE, JOHN BROOKS. "Crèvecoeur and Thoreau," *Papers of the Michigan Academy of Science, Arts and Letters,* V (1925), 309–33. An ill-tempered and inappropriate comparison that is nevertheless valuable for its occasional literary insights.

————. "The Rehabilitation of Crèvecoeur," *Sewanee Review,* XXXV (1927), 216–30. Analysis and appreciation of the realistic elements of the *Sketches.*

RAPPING, ELAYNE A. "Theory and Experience in Crèvecoeur's America," *American Quarterly,* XIX (1967), 707–18. Penetrating study of the operation of the ideas of natural order and human progress in the *Letters* and the *Voyage.*

RICE, HOWARD C. *Le Cultivateur Américain: Étude sur l'oeuvre de Saint John de Crèvecoeur.* Paris: Champion, 1932. An authoritative study of the evolution and influence of the *Lettres*; a ranging and informed work of scholarship.

————. "Some Notes . . . on the American Farmer's Letters," *Colophon,* Pt. XIX, No. 3 (1934). Summary of the above; chiefly valuable as the only report in English of its author's important research.

STONE, ALBERT E., JR. "Crèvecoeur's *Letters* and the Beginnings of an American Literature," *Emory University Quarterly,* XVIII (1962), 197–213. Best critical study of the *Letters*; thoughtful discussion of its relation to the development of American literature.

————. Foreword to *Letters from an American Farmer and Sketches of Eighteenth-Century America.* New York: New American Library, 1963. A version of the above essay.